The *DAO* of
HARMONY DAWN
COOKING

*Dearest Georgene
with love 💙
Nicola & Andy
Rosie 💙*

The *DAO* of
HARMONY DAWN COOKING

NICOLA LAWRENCE

THE DAO OF HARMONY DAWN COOKING

January 2007

The information in this book is true and complete to the best of my
knowledge. All recommendations are made without guarantee on the part
of the author.

Lawrence, Nicola 1962 Canada
The Dao of Harmony Dawn Cooking
"Innovative and Acclaimed Spa Cuisine"

Inquiries to the author can be directed to Harmony Dawn Retreat Centre,
www.harmonydawn.com

Dao begets one;
one begets two;
two begets three;
three begets all things.
All things are backed by the Shade (yin)
and faced by the Light (yang), and
harmonized by the immaterial Breath (ch'i)

PRAISE FOR HARMONY DAWN

From Retreat Attendees

"Whenever I am here I feel free. Free to explore the inner self. Thank you for creating and providing a safe and beautiful place for me to do this in. As always, the food that was prepared was exceptional. I am so happy that we found this place and the both of you." —**Paula E.**

"Thank you for the most wonderful weekend and for extending your vision to include others. Harmony Dawn is a loving, comforting place to unwind and rejuvenate. Your warmth and hospitality are appreciated." —**Dianne**

"Harmony Dawn – Natural Paradise: leopard frogs, migrating Canadian geese, white-tailed deer, setting suns, beavers, rising suns, pileated woodpeckers, humming windmills, trout lilies, babbling brooks, hawks, bubbling kettles, garter snakes, silence and laughter, big dippers, stillness and movement, solitude and companionship, orioles, new friends and old friends. Next time I will bring bigger pants." —**Steven Peck, President, Green Roofs for Healthy Cities**

"Form, function, beauty and warmth. Harmony Dawn is all this and more. A truly wonderful place, and a real privilege to share." —**Jeff**

"I loved the quiet, the soft water, the extraordinary sky, the harmony with nature and the soups, the curries and the granola, all of it…until next time" —**Elizabeth**

"I love this building and what it stands for. Your hospitality is unbeatable as is the food" —**Lisa**

"Harmony Dawn…the realization of dreams. Wisdom and compassion celebrated inside and out. Sunshine and wind, silence and laughter. Thank you for this most beautiful experience." —**Carrie**

"The experience of coming to Harmony Dawn has been truly reviving for me. I have found exactly what I needed to move forward in my life with a new, inspired sense of consciousness. Thank you from the bottom of my heart and soul." —**Jossilyn**

"Thank you so much for creating such a wonderful place for people to open their hearts and souls for such nurturing. I appreciate being able to come to Harmony Dawn and feel so welcomed, comfortable and at home. I hope to return very, very soon." —**Erin**

"In 30 years of leading retreats, I can truly say that the caring in the space and in the food has been without equal. Your mandala of merit continues to grow and to bless all those fortunate to come here." —**Catherine Jetsa Yeshe, Friends of the Heart**

"I have never felt so nourished in my life. I deeply thank you for those gifts that I can see and those that stay hidden from sight.
Till the next time." —**Gwen**

"If you two can do it, I can do it! What inspiration you provide through beauty, knowledge, humbleness and unabashed passion for the EARTH. I'm looking forward to returning to drink it all in." —**Sherri**

"I've fed my mind, body and spirit and ate like a goddess!" —**Nikki**

ACKNOWLEDGEMENTS

I am deeply grateful to all of my friends and family for their love and support over the last few years and to the following people who were instrumental in helping me bring this project to fruition.

First and foremost Sharon Buchanan, my book designer and dear friend of many years. This book would have been impossible without her tenacity, stubbornness, perfectionism, artistry and sheer will to complete this project against all personal odds, including my own. Neither of us realized what a phenomenally huge project we were undertaking.

Moira Nordholt for her superb culinary skills in designing our original menus and for her unwavering support, love and friendship.

My parents, Derek and Margaret, for their unbelievable support, their love of life and laughter and for teaching me how to cook.

My dear friends Pam and Dianna, for their incredible friendship and support over 20 years of growth, of cooking trials and much laughter. I love you both!

Andy James my soul mate, best friend and partner, who has a heart of gold and who is a constant inspiration. Together we built and are living a dream.

Shu wen, Shu wei and Hana for their love, sweetness, and for the promise of the future that we see in them.

Beryl James (Granny or Auntie Noo Noo) for her loveable disposition and her amazing culinary skills, which she has shared with me.

CONTENTS

BREAKFAST, BRUNCH & LUNCH

SALADS & SALAD DRESSING

SAUCES, DIPS & FUN STUFF

SOUPS & STEWS

ENTRÉES

DESSERTS

FOREWORD

THE DREAM OF HARMONY DAWN
By Andy James

Many guests have asked how Nicola and I came up with the vision of Harmony Dawn and how we went about building it. Here is our story!

The Dream

Harmony Dawn is a long-dreamt dream which suddenly blossomed into reality. Even as a teenager, I sometimes fantasized about a "dream house", the initial design of which featured rooms decorated in styles from all over the world so all cultures would be represented. During the 1970s, while living and studying in London, England, I became so excited by the newly emerging ideas on sustainable living, I seriously considered the possibilities of studying organic farming. In time, however, my enthusiasm for sustainability was gradually subdued by the grind of training and working as a Chartered Accountant during the day and in the evenings, pursuing my real passions - the Eastern martial arts, including taijiquan, and Buddhist Insight Meditation (vipassana). It seemed to me that if we wanted to effectively meet our mounting global challenges, we would have to learn to cooperate and trust on an unprecedented scale and this would involve individual transformation, which was what meditation was all about.

I married in 1975. In 1981, my wife Yolind and I moved to Toronto, expecting the first of our eventual three children. In 1983, my meditation teacher, Dhiravamsa, invited me to train with him as a Vipassana teacher, on beautiful San Juan Island, just across from Victoria, B.C. In spite of our precarious finances, we took the plunge and set off for the West coast! After a year, we moved back to Toronto so I could follow my heart in trying to become a teacher of meditation, taijiquan and qigong. Yolind and I separated in 1993 and the years that followed brought lots of turbulence and change in my life, although I was somehow able to continue my teaching with some success, founding "Tai Chi & Meditation Centres" (www.powerofbalance.com) in Toronto and Pickering.

In 1996, I read an article in The Toronto Star about the winner of the Toronto Healthy House competition, and was moved to visit it, especially since it was only two blocks away from my own Riverdale home. One Sunday, I took my three daughters on a tour of the unusual looking semi-detached house, located on a fairly small Toronto lot. I came away extremely impressed and excited by the advances that sustainable energy technology had made since the 1970s, when I last took serious notice. It was now not only workable but affordable!

I started to dream again and began to envision a sustainable, off-grid rural house that could function as an eventual retirement home, a legacy to my children and more immediately, a retreat centre. I knew something about retreats, having attended and then led them for nearly 25 years. This retreat would not just be a quiet place, but would play a positive part in guests' self-transformation process and would function as an experiential learning centre for sustainable energy technologies. People would get a chance to experience firsthand the possibilities and responsibilities of a greener future. I would also have an ideal space for conducting my own meditation, qigong, Taijiquan and other retreats.

The Dream Takes Form

My dreams remained mere imaginings until I met Nicola in 1998. I was surprised and amazed not only that she shared many of my general views on life but that she was genuinely excited by my vision of a rural retreat, even though we were both life-long "city people". In the spring of 1999, we decided, without any sense of urgency, to check out what kinds of rural property were up for sale around Toronto. At the very least, it would be an excuse to take road trips into the countryside which we both enjoyed. I calculated how far outside Toronto an hour and a half driving would take us and drew a semi-circle around Toronto on the map as our search area. We did not need the bottom half of the circle, since this would be in Lake Ontario.

At first, we mostly looked at properties with buildings, since this would be a cheaper option and would require far less work than building from scratch. Our ideal property would have a quiet, rural feel, preferably with no other buildings nearby and would be near some body of water – a lake, river or large pond. Both Nicola and I were familiar with Feng shui (the Qigong of the Earth), so the property should also have some Yin-yang balance, being neither too exposed nor enclosed, neither too hilly nor flat. Nothing we saw came even remotely close to our requirements even though we searched from Grey-Bruce in the West to

Belleville in the East. Many buildings were near major roads, mostly because (as we were to later learn) it is expensive to run power from the grid over longer distances; many could have starred in a movie of the book, Cold Comfort Farm. As soon as Nicola and I set eyes on the property which is now Harmony Dawn, we both immediately knew this was "The One", even though it was just overgrown meadows and woodlands. Something about its location and configuration just seemed right. By the end of August, 1999, we owned 50 plus acres of the Northumberland Hills, stretching down to Rice Lake, famous for its fishing and, in olden days, as an abundant and lush resource for native tribes.

In November 2000, we put in a culvert over our little stream in preparation for the time we might need a road up to our preferred building site. Even at this time, we had no immediate plans to build since the financing seemed impossible and anyway, there was no particular hurry. My best guess about the time frame for completing any type of building, even a small cottage by the lake, would have been about ten years.

However, the planetary currents had started to swirl, drawing us in. The first red flags Nicola and I noticed were America's withdrawal (shortly after George W. Bush became President in early 2001) from the Kyoto Protocol on global warming, the World Court and the 1972 Anti-ballistic Missile Treaty. September 11, 2001 convinced us the world was indeed in crisis and the need for healing refuges of the kind we envisioned, even though insignificant in global terms, was becoming much more urgent. We started looking for a sustainable energy designer and after some false starts, found Carolyn Moss, who was not only excited by our vision but was eager and able to help us realize it.

Initially, we envisioned three separate, inter-linked buildings which would consist of a kitchen-dining room pod, an accommodation pod and a studio-meeting room pod. These pods would be linked by walk-through green houses. Functionality and local building regulations soon impacted on our plans. We needed to make do with one building, not three, and the green houses proved impractical since they would need substantial southern exposure and would make the building too spread out. As a design feature, the greenhouses were added on to the southern part of the eventual building, and now function as a big "mud room" entrance and a quiet sunroom, suitable for reading and reflection. The building was still designed as three inter-linked pods, albeit within a single building.

In terms of the "look" of the building, we wanted it to be "normal". It should look and feel conventional because we did not want visitors to feel they had to be "weird" in order to embrace the wisdom of sustainable building and living.

Secondly, we wanted it to be "normal' in terms of the local environment. The central part of the building, incorporating the "tight and light" building principle, has a metal roof and its exterior is cedar-shingled, not unlike many buildings in the area. The flanking pods incorporate the "mass and glass" building principle of passive solar energy and look like garage add-ons…again not unlike some local buildings. The way the building functions, however, is much more efficient than the presently conventional.

Guest accommodation within the building is "shared" mainly for conservation reasons. Our conventional expectation of a single bedroom and bathroom for each person is extremely extravagant in terms of building costs, power and water (not to mention the extra cleaning and maintenance). We also thought the "sharing" aspect would be particularly appropriate at Harmony Dawn, which is a retreat centre catering to groups doing self-exploration, healing and team-building.

The last, but certainly not least, design factor was Feng shui. Yin-yang balance was a factor not only in determining the actual location of the building on the property but also in designing the building itself. It is also a central part of Nicola's cooking philosophy, as will be obvious in reading this book.

We broke ground in July 2002 and slogged through the crisis of Nicola's breast cancer, a brutally cold winter, many building setbacks and two trips a week out of Toronto, often with "Bear", my kids' dog. Somehow, we were ready for our official opening by the beginning of October 2003. On the actual day of our Grand Opening, we were blessed by a double rainbow over our building, which we named "Harmony Dawn". "Harmony" comes from the notion of dynamic balance or in other words, Yin-yang. "Dawn" alludes to my daughters' names, which share the word "Shu", meaning "dawn" in Chinese.

Living the Dream

In May, 2005, Nicola and I sold our Toronto home and moved full-time to Harmony Dawn. This represented a huge leap of faith since we did not know whether we would attract guests to our proposed retreat centre or how permanent country life would be for two "city folk" like Nicola and me. The transition and subsequent unfolding has been surprisingly smooth and most fulfilling. Shortly after we made our move, the number of retreat inquiries began to increase (because we had shifted our intent and energy) and by July, we were in full swing. Moira Nordholt, our first chef and dear friend, was invaluable not only in setting up our initial menus and starting us off with her kitchen genius, but in constantly encouraging us in our vision.

We do not miss the city, but more to the point, we love where we live, especially since we have been blessed by the greatest neighbours imaginable. The animals have grown to trust us and show themselves more and more. The land, water and sky are a constantly changing (and interactive) work of art.

Our guests have surpassed our expectations in many ways. Raving over the food is (initially surprising to us) the first and most common reaction. The special energy in the building and throughout the land is felt by many, including a well-known shaman from Quebec, who had powerful visions during her stay and communicated supportive messages from the local spirits and animals. She said we had placed our building in the centre of a giant "medicine wheel". Some of our guests feel inspired by the very fact that we had "walked our talk" and had actually turned our dream and vision into a reality. Some asked for more technical information so that they too could start living in a more sustainable manner; some groups have included idealistic young people from schools and universities, who will be the future caretakers of the planet. We have been repeatedly featured in the media and a weekend at Harmony Dawn was the first prize in a "One Tonne Challenge" emissions competition…before the government of Stephen Harper pulled the plug on funding, very shortly after he came to power.

For me (and also for Nicola), an unexpected gift has been meeting with spiritual teachers from many different traditions. In a different way, I had started reaching out beyond the boundaries of my own (Buddhist-Daoist) traditions by joining and working within the Forge Guild (www.theforge.org), a trans-traditional organization of spiritual teachers and leaders. Yet, here in our own home, gifted spiritual teachers were adding to the energy of our space and sharing their visions and teachings! Blessed Synchronicity indeed!

The Dao of Harmony Dawn Cooking

For many guests, the most immediate and striking feature of the Harmony Dawn experience is the food. The reason for this is obvious – Nicola, who pours her heart, intelligence, energy and intuition into her cooking.

Again, the main principle inspiring the cooking is the same one which runs throughout Harmony Dawn – harmonious balance that is suitable to each moment. I like to use the example of Taijiquan to explain Yin-yang in action because it is a mind-body discipline which is based on Yin-yang principles. These principles are valid whether you choose to use taijiquan as a martial art, a health exercise or an embodiment of spirituality. Within (skilled) Taijiquan, there is the balancing of many pairs of seeming opposites: inner-outer, heaven-earth, active-passive, substantial-insubstantial, form-formless etc. In order to develop true skill, which is what kungfu (gongfu) really means, one has to invest in practice and in knowledge, yet when the level of mastery is reached, everything seems effortless and free-flowing.

Nicola has studied Yin-yang theory in the context of Traditional Chinese Medicine (TCM), Feng shui and Taijiquan and has put that knowledge to good effect in her cooking. Yet yin-yang is not just the application of rigid principle because it acknowledges the constantly changing nature of our universe, which in turn requires spontaneity. We have to respond to the often surprising challenges of life, moment by moment.

Nicola's special ingredient, however, is love. She loves cooking and she loves people...and nurturing them. This energetic quality infuses her food and not only feeds us in a profound sense but opens us up so we drop our defences and allow ourselves to be nurtured.

One last thought about cooking. Carolyn Moss, our designer, recently attended one of Nicola's cooking workshops and related an interesting fact. She did a test to determine the size of her personal environmental "footprint" on the planet and discovered that the single best thing she could do (more than any environmental building strategies) was to switch to a vegetarian diet. Animal protein requires a lot more land, water and power than vegetable protein.

Dec. 20, 2006
Harmony Dawn

Andy James is the Founder of the Tai Chi & Meditation Centre and together with Nicola Lawrence manages Harmony Dawn Retreat. He is a spiritual teacher, martial artist, healer and author.

INTRODUCTION

HOW I CAME TO EMBRACE THE SPIRIT OF FOOD

My family came to Canada from Catford, England in the sixties bringing with us a very cockney British diet. Our meals were traditional and meat-orientated. Considering my parents at the time were not making much money, we existed on steak and kidney pie, liver and onions, white toast and of course, marmite, cheese sandwiches and roast beef (on Sundays). Did I mention that we also loved sweets, cakes and all things chocolaty?

We loved it and lived like that for many years until one day, in my early teens, my father read a book called "Sugar Blues" by William Dufty, a historical account of sugar from the 1500's to present day. I read it as well and, needless to say, it was, and still is, a shocking account of how white sugar, grown on the backs and with the blood of slaves, has altered our body chemistry and created many of our twentieth century diseases, earning the name "white death". The book is not for the faint of heart. I once lent it to a friend who became so paralyzed with fear and dread that she couldn't finish the book and was in shock for quite some time.

That book changed the lives of my family members and began our path to a healthier lifestyle. My father, without flinching, threw out everything in our kitchen that contained "white death". Having nothing left in the pantry, my parents quickly became regulars at the one and only "natural foods" store in Newmarket. Whole grains, honey, and all natural replacements were purchased. Back then, in the seventies, the organic health stores were simply called "natural", not "organic", because there were as yet no genetically modified foods, now called GMOs.

Over time, my appetite for chicken and red meat naturally declined, although I still ate a bit of seafood. I must admit that documentaries on the treatment of animals cultivated as food sources disturbed me, especially the widespread practice of injecting hormones and the manner in which animals were slaughtered. In my 20's, I decided to adopt a more vegetarian lifestyle and both my parents followed suit wholeheartedly. In fact, they joined the local vegetarian society and took pride in showing me all the new recipes that they were learning and enjoying with their new veggie friends…and thus the journey began.

At the age of 18, I started working in restaurants in various capacities (even when I held a full time job) because I was fascinated by food and the food service industry.

I loved to watch the various chefs prepare food and put toget[...] always loved baking, even as a child, and so it was especially re[...] real professionals put together a mouth-watering and scintillatir[...] the earliest recollections of my own baking experience were w[...] Left alone after school while both my parents worked, I would [...] kitchen baking cranberry bread, cookies or a cake, inspired by[...] for my family.

In 1989, my dear friend (and the designer of this book), Sharon [...], [...] to my home with a gift of a food magazine. She had been drawn to a particular photo of a salad while she was waiting for the train and was so taken with the textures and the colours, she could almost taste the dish. I thought, "Wow! I have never really looked at food in this way." From that point forward, I looked at food in my life in a new way. I started being more artistic with food and actually became so inspired that I decided to start my own catering company, called "Cate Butler". I was able to pursue my passions for cooking, catering and service through small functions and dinner parties all over the Toronto area. Eventually it became too much work for just one person, as I was actually juggling a career in production at an advertising agency and struggling with my personal relationship with my partner at the time.

Advertising gave me an unusual opportunity to see how food gets marketed and promoted. On one occasion, I became extremely disgusted and incensed when I realized they were actually hand picking live chickens, killing and then stuffing them in order to promote a pharmaceutical drug, which had absolutely nothing to do with chickens. Stuffed chickens were just part of a "catchy" tag line. I started paying more attention to the way animals are commonly used and abused by humans for personal gain. All of these realizations continued to transform the way I looked at the process of eating, the source of my food and the effect food had on my body. I found it impossible to remain in advertising, and with the demise of my personal relationship, I felt the need to break free of all structure and pursue something that had been in my heart for a very long time…Acting!

I quit my job and began working again in the food service industry, which gave me the freedom I so needed to take acting, speech and movement classes. I took anything that allowed me to express myself. Money was not a major consideration for me because I felt this overwhelming need for self expression. Eventually, my friend Rochelle Wilson, an acclaimed comedienne and actor, and I decided to do a play together for Summerworks Theatre Festival. I was excited and scared to death at the same time, having no stage experience, unlike Rochelle. I was haunted by a recurring dream of shaky legs on stage and not being able to get past my nerves. I decided to take Tai Chi classes, as I had read that it could help

...y get grounded in your legs and into the earth. My daily meditative walks, ...ng my lines, took me to the Tai Chi Chuan and Meditation studio on Danforth ...enue in Toronto and was my introduction to the Internal Arts, which opened ...ne up to a whole new world. This of course was where I met Andy, the man who would change my life forever in a very dynamic and passionate way.

Tai Chi Chuan really helped my acting. I went on to produce and star in another play with Rochelle for the Fringe Festival, secured roles in several commercials and a short film…not a star studded career by any standard, but fun and part of my journey. As my interest in the entertainment industry waned, my passion for the Internal Arts was gaining momentum and giving "balance" a whole new meaning. I studied Tai Chi Chuan, Qi Gong, Buddhism, Yin and Yang Theory, Feng Shui and Traditional Chinese Medicine (TCM). I was delighted to learn that food was regarded as an important aspect of Herbology, a branch of TCM. As my strength and experience in the martial arts grew, I began doing Feng Shui consultations privately and professionally, and taking a more serious look at cooking and in particular how that was affected by the notion of Ying-yang balance.

Andy and I had begun our journey together and with that blossomed the retreat centre. A dream for both of us, we began thinking about all the elements of our venture. I was in charge of Feng Shui, interior design and coordinating with our lovely friend, Moira Nordholt, on the menus and how to put the kitchen together. During the stressful building process, we were shocked to learn that I had breast cancer. We had a healthy lifestyle, ate well, worked out physically and spiritually and yet here I was with breast cancer! It was a transformative experience for me as I struggled to figure out why and how I got this disease. I began research on toxins and environmental concerns, and I became my own personal health advocate within the medical establishment. One of the most devastating facts I learned was that I am one of millions who unfortunately deal with breast cancer every year and the statistics are climbing rapidly. But why?

Andy and I began looking more carefully at our food sources and the "you are what you eat" adage, since we thought we had been eating right. I read many books and one in particular, really struck a chord. "A Call to Women", written by Sat Dharam Kaur, a Naturopathic doctor from Owen Sound, offered a wonderful program which helps women look at environmental, emotional and spiritual toxins and above all, food. So I took her course to learn as much as I could and at the same time, it gave me the opportunity to be accredited by her to teach her course, "The Healthy Breast Program", to other women.

I was healing and with that came the opening of the retreat centre. I felt an enormous sense of hope, peace and future, not just for Andy and our immediate family, but for others who were beginning to express interest. Surrounded by love and supported by many, it was the dawn of a new era in my life and in my cooking. Food now was more than just a matter of pleasing the palate. It was almost a spiritual path or "Dao".

Our Grand Opening was in 2003 and so far the response to our dream of Harmony Dawn has been overwhelming and positive. Many have come through our doors and expressed gratitude and love for what we have done for the environment and for how they themselves feel while they are here in our care, and on the land. One lady commented once that "if you had a disease and came here you would be healed".

There has also been tremendously positive feedback to the food at Harmony Dawn and to how I cook with guests regularly inquiring into how I put different elements together. Requests for recipes were so overwhelming I decided to write a book. This has been a tremendously validating and rewarding experience for me, which would not be possible without such support from guests, family and friends.

The Dao of Harmony Dawn Cooking is my own experience and journey, but it has been enriched by so many lovely people who have travelled with me along the way. Food has changed my life and taught me many lessons which now permeate my cooking. I try not only to please the eye and the taste buds but to help nourish body, psyche and spirit. Food in its most profound sense is not only the physical acts of cooking and eating, but it is also love, creativity and relationship.

The Politics of Food

Food has become a far more complex matter than it was two or even one hundred years ago, when production methods were simpler, choices were less and the links between producers and consumers much more direct. Food is now a global industry, driven by stock prices, competitive pricing (cheap food) and marketing, which can create or destroy demand. Instead of eating what our bodies need, most of us eat what is marketed to us…which means not only print and TV ads but the selection and presentation that is put before us on our supermarket shelves and in restaurants. Marketing is so powerful that if, for example, a certain type of fish becomes really fashionable, the global demand can be so immense that it can drive the species to the brink of extinction!

Ironically, the business of food has led to several developments which are actually detrimental to human health and well-being. The dictionary defines food as "a nutritious substance, especially solid in form, that can be taken into an animal or a plant to maintain life and growth". It is the basis of our life and deserves our most watchful attention. Unfortunately, most of us know little about our food except that it appears in our stores and restaurants. We do not know how our food is grown, processed, shipped or marketed. As a consequence of our ignorance or neglect, several disturbing developments have crept into food production and consumption.

The disturbing and indisputable fact is that the air we breathe, the water we use for drinking and irrigation, and the earth from which our food grows are poisoned with increasingly more complex chemicals, which are taking longer to break down. As a result, a (probably toxic) brew of pollutants is accumulating in our bodies and in the bodies of animals who live in even the remotest parts of our planet.

Many of these chemicals and hormones (and more recently, genetic modifications) are used in agriculture in order to produce "cheaper" (more profitable) and "better" (longer shelf life/more attractive appearance) food. The cumulative effect of the quality of our food intake cannot be underestimated since it is repetitive and taken directly into our bodies. Other pollutants (apart from the food industry) are the by-products of our modern lifestyle: drugs, shampoos, household cleaners, fire retardants and massive, diverse corporate waste and pollution etc. It is currently difficult (and impossibly expensive for ordinary individuals) to establish direct cause-and-effect between particular substances and their effect on individual people, so in the corridors of power, the prevailing view is that nothing is happening or if it is, no one is to blame. In our guts and in our hearts, however, most people know many things are going very wrong. Despite our prosperity, our hospitals are overflowing. We are intricately connected with the Earth and ignore that fact at our peril.

The rapidly rising rate of cancer in both humans and animals is a strong indication that something is wrong with our environment. Thirty years ago, the World Health Organization declared that up to 90% of all cancers are caused by pesticides, radiation, and other toxic chemicals in our environment. Dr. Samuel Epstein, whose research was key in banning DDT, pointed out that all of us now carry more than 500 different compounds in our cells, none of which existed before 1920 and that "there is no safe dose for any of them". Rachel Carson, a marine biologist, ecologist, environmentalist, writer and activist, was one of the pioneers of the environmental movement in the 60's with her book Silent Spring, which drew attention to the toxic changes in our environment. Rachel Carson succumbed to breast cancer in 1964 at the age of 57.

In the summer of 2005, the Toronto Star featured an article by acclaimed naturalist artist Robert Bateman titled "I am Canadian and I am polluted". He had volunteered for the Toxic Nation project, which was a ground-breaking attempt to analyze the level of pollution in Canadians (www.ToxicNation.ca). They tested blood and urine from men and women of varying ages, backgrounds and regional neighbourhoods and discovered that all participants had on average 44 of the 88 chemicals tested. Of these 88 chemicals, 53 caused reproductive disorders and harmed the development of children, 41 were suspected of causing cancer, 27 disrupted the hormonal system and 21 were associated with respiratory illnesses. In our Global Village, pollution knows no boundaries and covers the greatest of distances.

One of the most powerful factors driving the food industry is the concept of "fast" or "convenience" foods. The time constraints on our busy lives make it difficult to provide healthy, wholesome and nutritious meals for ourselves and our families and so not surprisingly, processed and packaged foods become attractive. The marketers are now even touting TV dinners as some kind of gourmet dining! A recent study in the Toronto Star found that daily meal preparation time in 1900 was six hours; in 1990 it was 1 hour; in 2005 it decreased to a paltry 20 minutes. To me, this means more processing, additives, and packaging, but less human interaction in the age-old process of preparing and sharing food in a communal situation.

Another aspect of the fast food industry which is only just coming to public awareness is that, apart from all the chemical and hormonal additives along the food production chain, the final products are doused in liberal amounts of fats, sugar and salt. These are not only addictive but trigger all sorts of health problems, including obesity. A couple of facts of which you may not be aware – girls are starting to menstruate as young as 7 and 8, probably as a result of the prolonged use of growth hormones in animals, milk etc. Many morticians do not embalm bodies anymore because of all the preservatives ingested over a lifetime.

Genetically Modified Foods (GMO's)

GMO's are plants or animals which have been genetically engineered or modified. Most of the foods that you presently see in an average supermarket are GMO's. In the early 90's when GMOs were first introduced within North America, they were proudly marketed as a new kind of high-tech food and were met with overwhelming rejection by the general public, giving rise to the derogative term, "frankenfoods". The big corporations in Canada and America promptly did a strategic u-turn and lobbied their respective governments to be able to market GMO's alongside traditional produce without having to label their produce as GMO's or in any way as different. Since Canada and the USA, along with Australia, were in the forefront of this new industry and since GMO industry players included enormous companies like Monsanto, they succeeded, certainly within North America and perhaps worldwide, although there is far more spirited resistance in

Europe. In North America, they have prevailed despite clear and persistent public resistance…which somehow does not seem to be in the spirit of democracy.

Lest you underestimate the power of Big Business, I suggest you see the wonderful and informative Canadian-made movie, "The Corporation", which offers a sober, historical account of how corporate greed has swelled to psychopathic proportions (certainly in North America) and is affecting our lives, including our global food supply.

One of the most touching and gut-wrenching GMO stories is the legal battle between Percy Schmeiser and Monsanto, which has gone as far as the Supreme Court in Canada. Percy Schmeiser is a third generation, 75 year old farmer, who has been sued by the goliath Monsanto, because Monsanto GMO plants were found growing in a ditch next to his fields. Although Schmeiser had scrupulously been developing and saving his own seeds for over 50 years and the most likely explanation for the plants is seeds blowing in the wind (who would have thought?). The courts, even in appeal, have found against Schmeiser! Much of the legal argument turns on the legal ability to patent various forms of life. A huge, related issue at stake is the right to develop your own seeds. For more on Schmeiser, see the article in Common Ground magazine, January 2004, or just 'Google' him up. Monsanto is powerful and well connected politically and they will try to have us believe that genetic engineering is all about feeding the hungry and about protecting the environment. But this is the same company that brought us Agent Orange, PCB's and bovine growth hormone. Hmmm.

We are the keepers of the Earth. It is up to our generation to ensure that the planet can sustain and support life without endangering ourselves or all the creatures that inhabit the earth. We need to have a loud (any will do) voice and to speak out against these vile atrocities that threaten our well-being and that of our children.

Food is big business, controlled by the FDA, the Food and Drug Association in the United States. The line between drugs and food is quite blurred. We need to reconnect with the earth, with ourselves and in doing so, reclaim our food supply. For a detailed list of GMO's and where they hide, check Greenpeace's web site.

What can we do?

Although we may feel helpless, we can influence the marketplace in a simple way through our spending habits, all of which are carefully taken into account by market researchers. It also helps to discuss these matters with the people we meet…whether servers in our local stores, friends or influential people.

One of the most immediate things we can do is to start buying "organic".

Although it is becoming more fashionable for people to purchase only organic food, a surprising number refuse to purchase anything "organic" on principle, even if the price is competitive, or actually cheaper. The latter feel that "organic food" is a conspiracy of sorts…a theory that I personally have heard several times during my many supermarket adventures. The reasons for buying organic have been explained above. A caution – many people, including some GMO producers, are trying to sneak their products under the "organic" label even if they are not, so read your labels carefully and if you find some tricksters, raise a stink!

Another way we can help ourselves is to buy "local" whenever possible and do our best to inquire into the conditions in which plants and animals are raised. Many supermarket chains today are locked into lengthy, year-round contracts with big industry. Within North America, California and Florida farms often beat out local farmers with their cheaper (often highly fertilized and pesticide laden) produce, even at the height of the local growing season. This happens in our own area which is surrounded by farmers and fields. It is not unusual to go into local supermarkets during the summer and not find Ontario produce! Nowadays you can purchase goods year round from countries all around the world. In most cases, unless organic, we really do not know how the food is grown or how the animals are treated…and many people probably do not want to know.

My own motto is "support our local farmers". They work so hard producing vegetables and fruit in our short growing season and for such little recognition and monetary return. They are connected to the earth and know the hardships that impact the earth and the growing cycle. Global warming has produced flash floods, droughts, and tornado like conditions that devastate the landscape. Yet they keep going and growing. There is something about the spirit of the farmer that resonates in my soul…when in my own garden in summer, I hold in my hands the bounty that comes from organic earth, bright sunshine, and fresh rainfall; when I take a moment to feel the natural creases in a tomato or smell the freshness of herbs and see from one day to the next how fast a zucchini can mature or how long it takes to cultivate a butternut squash. When I put them on the table, they require nothing short of themselves to be a taste extravaganza. This is an important part of macrobiotic cooking – eating local produce in season, so that the natural flavours can explode on our taste buds without needing to be boosted by large amounts of salt, sugar or spices.

Yin and Yang of Harmony Dawn Cooking

An integral part of macrobiotic theory (and my own cooking philosophy) is the Chinese concept of Yin and Yang – seemingly opposite yet complementary natural forces that create an orderly, balanced universe. Yin and yang are difficult to describe in Western terms, because they are energetic concepts, not tangible objects. The way yin and yang interact regulates every dimension of life from the spiritual to the physical. Nothing is exclusively yin or yang; both forces exist in all things.

Macrobiotics classifies each food as yin or yang in relation to other foods. In other words, yin and yang are relative rather than absolute concepts. Whether a food is relatively more yin or more yang depends on a variety of factors, including where it was grown, its mineral and water contents, color, texture, taste and effect on the body. Whole grains and most vegetables fall near the midpoint between yin and yang, making them nourishing mainstays of the macrobiotic diet. Sugar, refined foods and stimulants like coffee and chocolate are considered highly yin, causing energy imbalances, nervousness, worry and lack of focus. Red meats, cheese and refined salt are believed to be especially yang producing tight muscles, congestion, and tending us towards hostility and criticism.

Macrobiotic practitioners generally design meals to produce a yin-yang balance while avoiding extremes in individual foods. Though foods at opposite ends of the continuum (chocolate cake and steak, for instance) do balance one another, eating such extreme yin and yang foods causes physiological and psychological stresses, according to the macrobiotic doctrine. Selecting more balanced foods promotes physical and mental vitality, equilibrium and a positive outlook. It also reduces craving, which is a sign of imbalance.

HOW TO USE MY BOOK

Although all my recipes are tested, the only ones that should be followed exactly are baked goods and desserts. All other recipes in the book are meant as guides only. Follow them as I have laid them out and use taste tests along the way to achieve the taste and flavour you want. Cooking is meant to be fun and also something that is creative and self expressive.

The Harmony Dawn Pantry and Kitchen Notes

All of the ingredients and staples you will need can be found in most supermarkets, Asian markets, specialty markets or natural/health food stores. All recipes are made using all organic products. Use organic Ontario produce or your local farmer (where possible), organic unrefined sugars, organic unbleached/unrefined flours, organic whole grains, seeds and herbs and wild fish. The following lists the ingredients you will need when using my book.

Dried Beans or Legumes

Canned beans are an easy substitute and quick to have on hand but cooking dried beans is always preferable. They are loaded with vitamins, minerals and protein.

Chickpeas, cannellini beans, navy beans, great Northern beans, black beans, kidney beans~white and red, soybeans, adzuki beans, yellow and green split peas, lentils~brown, green, red, french puy.

Grains & Flour

Brown rice, millet, quinoa, bulgur, couscous, Thai black rice, red rice, basmati rice, rolled oats, whole wheat bread and pastry flour, all-purpose flour, spelt flour, buckwheat flour, rye flour, brown rice flour, potato flour, wheat bran, wheat germ.

Baking

Baking soda, non aluminum baking powder, active dry yeast, yellow and blue cornmeal, dutch cocoa, carob powder, chocolate chips or semi sweet chocolate, carob chips, crystallized ginger, pure extracts~vanilla, almond, mint, coconut, orange, cinnamon sticks, graham crackers, Xanthan gum, guar gum.

Sweeteners

Honey, maple syrup, brown rice syrup, barley malt syrup, Sucanet, unrefined molasses, dates, applesauce, unrefined cane sugar.

Thickeners

Tahini, kudzu, arrowroot, cornstarch.

Dried Fruits, Nuts & Seeds

Thompson raisins, sultanas, currants, dried cranberries, dried blueberries, apricots, dried apples, dates, figs, sunflower seeds, pumpkin seeds, flax seeds, white and black sesame seeds, almonds, walnuts, pine nuts, cashews, pecans, shredded coconut, hazelnuts, peanuts.

Oils & Vinegars

Toasted sesame oil, unrefined sesame oil, sunflower oil, olive oil, extra virgin olive oil, walnut oil, grapeseed oil, good quality balsamic vinegar, fig and raspberry vinegar, tarragon vinegar, umeboshi vinegar, apple cider vinegar, rice wine vinegar, red and white wine vinegar.

Condiments

Tamari, Bragg Liquid Aminos*, mirin, soy sauce, kecap manis, misos ~ light, dark and buckwheat, vegetarian hoisin sauce, sambal oelek, chili oil, black bean sauce, umeboshi paste, pickled ginger, green and red curry paste, chili sauce, chipotles in adobo sauce, horseradish, fine and coarse sea salt, vegetable salt, dijon and hot mustard, mayonnaise, nayonnaise, sundried tomatoes, black and green olives, cooking sherry, dried shiitake mushrooms, nutritional yeast, organic tahini, organic peanut and almond butter, vegetable stock cubes, wasabi powder, liquid smoke.

* Throughout this book Bragg Liquid Aminos are referred to solely as "Braggs"

Sea Vegetables

Dulse, arame, kombu, hijiki and nori.

Dried Herbs & Spices

Try to use fresh garden herbs wherever possible but dried herbs are a good substitute. Storage life should be checked periodically as they lose their potency after a couple of months.

Basil, oregano, rosemary, paprika, sweet paprika, chili powder, bay leaves, dill, tarragon, coriander, cumin, garam masala, dried red chili flakes*, curry powder, cayenne, turmeric, caraway seeds, fennel seeds, marjoram, sage, thyme, herbes de Provence, mustard powder, onion and garlic powder, Chinese 5 spice powder, Tohami Togarashi chilies, cinnamon, nutmeg, cardamom, allspice, cloves, ginger, anise seeds.

*Throughout this book dried red chili flakes are referred to solely as dried chilies

Miscellaneous

Organic tempeh and tofu, pesto sauce, tomato sauce, canned tomatoes, soba noodles, kamut noodles, whole grain pasta, rice noodles, kaffir lime leaves, soy milk, organic cow's milk, eggs, cream, butter, buttermilk, almond milk, brown rice crispies, frozen puff pastry.

Equipment

Good knives, cutting boards, baking sheets, muffin tins, bread pans, cake tins, pie plates, cheesecake pan, casserole dish, pots of various sizes, frying pan, stove top to oven skillet, spatulas, measuring cups and spoons, can opener, wooden mixing spoons, mixing bowls of various sizes, garlic press, food processor or blender, KitchenAid mixer (not necessary but a luxury), rice cooker, strainers, potato masher, vegetable peeler, rolling pin, metal graters, colander, cooling racks.

Measurements & Temperature

Oven cooking temperatures are in Fahrenheit and based on a regular cooking oven. If you have a convection oven, decrease oven temperature by approximately 50 degrees.

All measurements used are U.S. standard.
Common abbreviations used throughout the book are:

tsp = teaspoon	1 stick of butter = 8 tbsp = ½ cup
tbsp = tablespoon	lb = pound

Measurement Equivalents and Metric Conversions

U.S. Measurements

3 tsp	=	1 tbsp
4 tbsp	=	¼ cup
16 tbsp	=	1 cup

Volume (Liquid)

4 oz	=	½ cup		
8 oz	=	1 cup	=	½ pint
16 oz	=	2 cups	=	1 pint
32 oz	=	4 cups	=	1 quart

Metric Conversion

1 tsp	=	5 ml		
3 tsp	=	1 tbsp	=	15 ml
¼ cup	=	59.1 ml		
½ cup	=	118.3 ml		
1 cup	=	240 ml	=	¼ litre

Volume

1 cup	=	250 ml		
4 cups	=	1000 ml	=	1 litre

Weight

1 oz	=	30 grams
½ lb	=	225 grams
1 lb	=	450 grams
2.2 lb	=	1 kg

A Note About Vegan Cooking

Many of the recipes in my book are vegan, which means they do not use ingredients that are derived from animals. Butter, milk and milk products, animal meats and honey are usually not eaten in a vegan diet. If there is a specific recipe that contains any of these items, they can easily be substituted with vegan margarine (available at health food stores), soy/rice/almond milk, soy cheese and maple syrup.

1
BAKED GOODS

Basic Oatmeal Muffins

1 healthy dozen

> Well here it is! I have been asked so many times for this recipe. They are easy and always a hit. I think the real secret to success is to throw in whatever you have on hand at the moment. Substitute spelt flour if you are sensitive, yoghurt or soy milk for the buttermilk. Have them plain or add any of the additions for customized muffins.

Muffins require a very hot oven and short baking times. Preheat oven to 400° and have ready, lightly oiled muffin tins.

1½ cups	rolled oats
1½ cups	buttermilk
¾ cup	melted butter or safflower oil
½ cup	honey
2	eggs, whisked
1½ cups	whole wheat flour
1½ tsp	sea salt
¾ tsp	baking soda
1½ tsp	baking powder

In a large bowl combine the oats and the buttermilk and let sit for 15 minutes or overnight. Using a wooden spoon, stir in the oil/butter, honey and eggs, blending well one ingredient at a time.

In a separate bowl, sift the dry ingredients together. Stir the dry ingredients into the wet ingredients until just mixed, adding any of the additions if desired. Do not over mix batter.

Spoon the batter into the muffin tins and bake for 20 to 25 minutes. Let them cool in the pan for 5 minutes then remove.

Optional Additions:

1. 1½ cups of peeled chopped apples with 1½ tsp each of cinnamon and freshly grated nutmeg.

2. ¾ cup of chopped dates with 2 tsp orange zest and a pinch of ground cloves.

3. ¾ cup of chopped, toasted pecans, ¾ cup of fresh cranberries, 2 tsp of orange zest.

4. 1½ cups of fresh, wild blueberries with 2 tsp of lemon zest.

5. ¾ cup of toasted, chopped walnuts, ¾ cup of peeled, chopped apples, 1½ tsp of cinnamon.

6. ¾ cup of diced banana, ¾ cup dried cranberries and 1 tsp each of orange and lemon zest.

7. ¾ cup carob chips with ¾ cup toasted, chopped walnuts.

8. 1½ cups dried cherries, 1 tsp fresh ground cardamom and 1 tsp orange zest.

9. 1½ cups mixed toasted seeds, pumpkin, sunflower and sesame with 2 tsp mace.

10. ¾ cup chocolate chips and ¾ cup diced banana, 1 tsp vanilla extract.

CHEF'S TIP:

Quick breads such as muffins, require that you merely combine the batter. By over blending, the gluten in the flour is activated and the muffins will not rise. If there are a few white lumps, that is okay, they will disappear when baked.

Sunshine Morning Muffins

1 healthy dozen

" These muffins were inspired by my very good friend and chef Moira Nordholt. We made these muffins early one Saturday morning for a group. We just threw in what we had on hand and they were a hit. Dense, moist, spirited, great for digestion and vegan! "

1½	ripe bananas	½ cup	chopped dates
½ cup	cranberry juice	1 tsp	baking powder
1 tsp	pure vanilla extract	½ tsp	sea salt
½ cup	maple syrup	½ tsp	baking soda
1 cup	whole wheat flour	1 tsp	cinnamon
¾ cup	organic oats	½ tsp	nutmeg
½ cup	wheat bran	½ cup	sunflower seeds

Lightly oil muffin tins and set aside. Preheat oven to 360°.

In a large bowl mash the bananas until smooth. Add the cranberry juice, vanilla and maple syrup. Blend well. Stir in oats.

In a separate bowl, combine remaining ingredients except the sunflower seeds. Add the dry ingredients to the wet and blend until just combined. Do not over mix. Spoon into the muffin tins and sprinkle with the sunflower seeds.

Bake for 20-25 minutes. Let rest in tin for 5 minutes and then cool on racks.

Savoury Blue Corn Muffins

Makes 12 muffins

These muffins have a funky, blue colour and they are especially good with a hearty soup in the middle of winter. Substitute spelt flour or whole wheat for the all-purpose and yoghurt or soy milk for the buttermilk. Substitute brown sugar for the sucanet if unavailable.

1½ cups	blue cornmeal		¼ cup	onion, minced
1 cup	all-purpose flour		1 clove	garlic, minced
1 tsp	sea salt		2	eggs, whisked
1 tbsp	baking powder		1 cup	buttermilk
2 tbsp	sucanet		½ cup	roasted bell peppers
¾ cup	unsalted butter, melted		2 tbsp	chopped parsley

Optional: ¾ cup grated Parmesan cheese

Butter muffin tins and set aside. Preheat oven to 400°.

In a bowl stir together the cornmeal, flour, salt, baking power, sucanet and cheese if using. In another bowl whisk together the butter, onion, garlic, eggs, buttermilk, chopped roasted peppers and parsley. Stir into the flour mixture until just combined.

Pour into muffin tins and bake in the middle of the oven for approximately 18 minutes or until golden. Let sit in tin for 5 minutes and then promptly remove.

CHEF'S TIP:

To roast peppers. Set oven on broil, place peppers on an oiled baking sheet. Turn peppers as each side becomes charred. When fully charred, remove, place in a covered bowl to steam. When cool, remove skin and seeds.

Cranberry Orange Scones

16 generous pie shaped scones

These scones are rich and flaky with the sweetness coming from the cranberry juice and a touch of maple syrup. Serve warm with homemade preserves. Use a combination of white, whole wheat or spelt, if desired.

4 cups	all-purpose flour	½ cup	cranberry juice
1 cup	organic oats	½ cup	maple syrup
1 tsp	baking soda	½ cup	buttermilk
3 tsp	baking powder	1 cup	dried cranberries
¾ cup	chilled unsalted butter, cut into bits	2 tbsp	cream
			Zest and juice of one orange

Combine all dry ingredients. Cut in the butter using fingers, a pastry cutter, or two knives until it resembles coarse meal and is crumbly.

In another bowl combine all wet ingredients.

Make a well in the centre of the dry ingredients and pour the wet mixture into the centre. Begin by blending with a wooden spoon until just combined. Turn onto a floured surface and gently knead for a minute until you have a nice smooth patty, you may need to add more flour if too wet.

Using a rolling pin, roll the dough out to a ¾ inch smooth round patty and cut into pie shapes or use a round cookie cutter to make circular scones.

Place scones on a parchment paper lined baking sheet, brush with cream and bake at 400° for 10 to 15 minutes or until puffy and golden.

Dill & Cheddar Scones

Makes about 24 scones

Perfect with soup, eggs, or afternoon tea. Serve with a little bit of butter and extra cheddar cheese. Chipotle peppers have a lovely smoky, hot flavour. They are sold in small cans with adobo sauce.

2 cups	all-purpose flour	½ cup	unsalted butter
¾ tsp	sea salt	1 cup	strong cheddar, grated
1 tbsp	baking powder	1 tsp	freshly ground pepper
2	eggs, beaten	½ cup	light cream
¼ cup	fresh dill, chopped		

Optional: 1 tbsp puréed chipotle peppers

Preheat oven to 450°.

In a large bowl, stir together flour, baking powder, salt, pepper and dill. Cut in the butter using fingers, a pastry cutter or two knives until the mixture resembles coarse meal. Add cheddar.

In a small bowl, mix together the eggs, cream and chipotles if using. Make a well in the centre of the flour mixture and add the eggs and cream. Stir together to make a soft, sticky dough.

Turn dough onto a lightly floured surface and knead until it holds together. You may need additional flour. Roll out the dough to a ½ inch thick patty and using a cookie cutter, cut into circles 1 to 3 inches in width. Place on a baking sheet lined with parchment and brush tops with a little extra cream. Bake for 10 minutes, until golden.

Basics of Bread Making

Bread making is satisfying and rewarding. A common misconception is that it is time consuming and labour intensive. Actually, most of the time is spent waiting for the dough to rise.

Proofing the Yeast:

Yeast is the living organism that converts the natural sugars in flour to gases. Proofing, ensures that the yeast is alive. The water temperature is critical, it should be warm enough to activate the yeast but not so hot that it kills it. Between 105 and 110 degrees or comfortable to the touch.

Make the Dough:

Mix the proofed yeast with the liquid, salt and oil that are called for in the recipe, then gradually add the flour, stirring with a wooden spoon until dough pulls away from sides of bowl.

Knead the Dough:

Kneading completes the mixing process, it allows the flour's protein to develop into gluten. Knead until springy, about 10 minutes.

Rising:

Most doughs rise in 1-2 hours. During this period the yeast multiplies and the gluten in the flour begins to stretch and strengthen. Fermentation begins. In the absence of oxygen the yeast organisms begin to break the starch down into simple sugars. This yields carbon dioxide gas, which leavens the dough. Too long a rise will weaken the gluten structure and cause it to collapse. It is ready when the dough springs back slowly.

Turn out onto floured surface and knead gently about 5 times to release the built up carbon dioxide and to reinvigorate the yeast and gluten. Form into a ball and let rise uncovered another 5-10 minutes.

Shape and Rise Again:

Shape the dough according to recipe and let rise again. The second takes less than the first, about 45 minutes because the gluten has already formed. Make several slashes in the top of loaf with a sharp knife. The slashes will allow the dough to expand rapidly without tearing. You can brush on the glaze, such as beaten egg, or sprinkle with seeds at this time.

Bread Ingredients:

Basic ingredients are flour, water and yeast. Adding oil, butter and eggs will give the dough a soft tender texture and deeper flavour. Salt is used to add flavour and control the rate of fermentation.

Glazing:

There are different ingredients you can use to glaze bread and rolls, each will produce a different outcome to the final product. Melted butter gives a nice soft crust, milk makes a nice brown crust and beaten egg will make the bread shine.

Wheat Free Bread:

Gluten is absent in spelt, kamut and other non-wheat flours. It is what helps bread rise. Xanthan gum and guar gum (both sold in health food stores) will help bind these flours making them lighter and rise better. Adding 1 tbsp per cup or so of flour will suffice.

Basic Whole Wheat Bread

Makes four 8 x 4 inch loaves

> Baking bread is a rewarding and primal experience, connecting us with our ancestors and thousands of years of breaking bread with our fellow man. Kneading, rising, letting it rest, and finally, what can feel like hours later, baking. That unmistakable aroma fills the air, the crowd appears, and the bread is devoured in minutes.

4 cups	warm water, 110°
3 tbsp	active dry yeast
3 tbsp	honey
1 tbsp	sea salt
4 cups	all-purpose flour
4 cups	whole wheat, or spelt flour
2 tbsp	unsalted butter, melted

Optional: combine ½ cup oats, ¼ cup flax seeds and ¼ cup sesame seeds

Lightly oil four bread pans and set aside.

In a large bowl, combine the warm water, yeast and the honey. Stir and let sit for about 10 minutes until the yeast is foamy. Add the salt.

Using a wooden spoon, begin adding the flour, 2 cups at a time. Add 2 cups white and then 2 cups whole wheat, blending well after each addition. When you think you can't mix any more, turn the dough onto a floured surface and start kneading, adding additional flour as needed. Knead for about 10 minutes until you have a firm but elastic dough.

Put dough into a lightly oiled bowl covered with a towel or plastic wrap and let rise in a warm place for about an hour, until doubled in size. Punch the dough down, turn out onto a lightly floured surface and form into loaves.

Optional: roll the loaves in the oat, seed combination.

Place in loaf pans, cover and let rise again for approximately 30 to 45 minutes, or until doubled. Brush with melted butter and bake in a preheated 350° oven for 30 minutes until golden and sounds hollow when tapped with a wooden spoon.

Oatmeal Molasses Bread

Makes four 8 x 4 inch loaves

This is a very dense bread and it is excellent toasted.

4 cups	boiling water		2 tbsp	unsalted butter, melted
2 cups	organic oats		1 cup	molasses
1 cup	warm water, 110°		5 cups	whole wheat flour
1 tsp	honey		5 cups	all-purpose flour
3 tbsp	active dry yeast		1 tbsp	sea salt

Lightly oil 4 bread pans and set aside.

In a large bowl pour the boiling water over the oatmeal, stir to blend and let stand for 20 minutes until cooled slightly.

In a small bowl mix the warm water with the honey and yeast, let stand until foamy, about 10 minutes.

To the oatmeal mixture add the melted butter, molasses, salt and yeast mixture. Begin adding flour, 2 cups whole wheat, 2 cups white and mix until you can no longer mix. Turn onto a floured surface and begin kneading, adding additional flour as needed. Knead for about 10 minutes until you have a firm but elastic dough. Cover with plastic wrap or a towel and let rise in a warm place until doubled, approximately 1-1½ hours.

Punch the dough down and turn onto a floured surface and form into loaves. Sprinkle oats on top of loaves and place in prepared pans. Cover and let rise again for approximately 30 minutes, until doubled in size.

Bake in a preheated 400° oven for 15 minutes and then reduce the heat to 350° and continue baking for another 25 minutes until the loaves sound hollow when tapped.

A Cautionary Tail About Oatmeal Bread

Be warned that this yummy recipe can unleash unrestrained appetites! After one retreat, we had come back to Toronto with our big loveable dog Bearsie. We unloaded Bearsie and our bags (containing 2 loaves of oatmeal molasses bread) at our front door and went around the back to put the car away.

Upon returning minutes later we noticed some crumbs and liquid on the floor and wondered what it could be. A rather sheepish, 130 lb dog cowering behind the table gave us a clue. Bearsie, who is normally extraordinarily restrained and well mannered couldn't resist the aroma of the loaves and had extracted them from the plastic bags, removed the saran wrap and had wolfed down both loaves in a matter of seconds, much to his delight, leaving us with just a few crumbs!

Potato Onion Bread

Makes two 9 x 5 inch loaves

This is a fabulous winter bread. It is full of flavour and pairs well with a hearty soup or a big slice of cheddar cheese. Serve warm or toasted for maximum taste sensation.

2 tbsp	active dry yeast		1 tbsp	caraway seeds
½ cup	warm water, 110°		2 cups	boiling water
2 cups	onions, chopped fine		1 cup	potato flour
3 tbsp	molasses		4 cups	spelt flour
1 tbsp	sea salt		4 cups	rye flour
3 tbsp	sunflower oil		1 cup	sunflower seeds

In a small bowl combine the warm water, yeast, a touch of molasses and let stand for 10 minutes until foamy.

Using a stand up mixer with a dough hook, combine the onions, molasses, salt, oil, caraway seeds and sunflower seeds (alternatively mix by hand in a large mixing bowl). Add the yeast mixture, potato flour, 2 cups of the spelt flour and beat for 5 minutes. Add the rye flour and enough remaining spelt flour to make a stiff dough.

Knead the dough on a lightly floured surface for 10 to 15 minutes, using more spelt flour to prevent sticking.

Place the dough in a lightly oiled bowl, cover and let rise in a warm place until doubled in size, approximately 1 hour. Punch the dough down, shape into 2 loaves, roll in additional sunflower seeds and place in oiled loaf pans. Cover and let rise another 30 minutes.

Bake in a preheated 375° oven for 40 to 45 minutes. Bread will sound hollow when tapped.

Pizza Dough

Makes a 15 inch round pizza or an 11 x 15 rectangle

Pizza dough is super easy and fun to make. I always like to have dough on hand so I freeze it and then defrost it in the refrigerator. Bring to room temperature and then proceed with the recipe. Substitute all spelt if you are intolerant to wheat.

1 cup	warm water, 110°		1 tsp	sea salt
2 tbsp	honey		1 cup	whole wheat flour
1 tsp	active dry yeast		1½ cups	white bread flour
2 tbsp	olive oil			

In a large bowl, dissolve the honey in the warm water, add the yeast and let stand 10 to 15 minutes until foamy.

Add the oil, salt and whole wheat flour and stir using a wooden spoon. Add the remaining white flour and blend until the dough is firm but soft and you can move it to a floured surface.

Knead for 5 minutes or so adding more flour to prevent sticking, if necessary. Place dough in a lightly oiled bowl, cover with a towel and let rise in a warm spot for 1½ hours. Punch down. Let rest for 5 minutes and then place on lightly oiled baking sheet or pizza wheel and stretch to fit pan. If you feel resistance, let dough rest a few minutes and then proceed with your favourite pizza recipe.

CHEF'S TIP:

Add ½ cup chopped sundried tomatoes or olives with ½ cup chopped rosemary to the flour mixture. Or add ½ cup chopped thyme or a combination of thyme and sage to the flour mixture.

Honey Almond Bread

Makes two large 9 x 5 inch loaves

" I love this bread, it tastes amazing, but more importantly it is easy to make. Light, fragrant and sweet, it can be enjoyed toasted with jam or served warm with afternoon tea. Use all whole wheat or spelt flour if you prefer. "

3 tbsp	active dry yeast	3 cups	whole wheat flour
½ cup	warm water, 110°	3 cups	white bread flour
⅔ cup	honey, plus 1 tsp	⅔ cup	almond slices
¼ cup	unsalted butter	1 cup	raisins
2 cups	buttermilk	1	egg, whisked
2 tsp	sea salt		

Lightly oil two 9 x 5 inch bread pans.

In a small bowl mix the yeast, a teaspoon of honey and the warm water and let stand until foamy, about 10 minutes.

Meanwhile in a saucepan over low heat, melt the butter with the honey. Remove from heat and add the salt, buttermilk and raisins.

In a large bowl combine the butter mixture and the yeast. Add the whole wheat flour, ½ of the almond slices and stir until well blended with no lumps. Add the white flour ½ cup at a time until you can't mix anymore. Turn out onto a lightly floured surface and begin kneading, adding additional white flour until you have a firm but slightly sticky dough. Place in a lightly oiled bowl and leave in a warm place covered with a damp tea towel for one hour or until doubled in size.

Punch the dough down and let rest in the bowl for a minute or two. Turn out onto lightly floured surface and knead for 2 minutes. Divide the dough in half and shape into loaves. Cover and let rise another 45 minutes to an hour until doubled in volume. Preheat oven to 375°.

Brush the top of the loaves with the egg and sprinkle with remaining almond slices. Bake for approximately 45 minutes or until a deep gold in color. Let the bread cool for 5 minutes, remove from pan and cool on a rack.

Sundried Tomato Foccacia Bread

Serves 12-15 (makes enough to fill a 15 x 10 inch pan)

" This bread is without a doubt the most popular at Harmony Dawn. The aroma of roasting garlic and rosemary are just too irresistible for words. It is great with a little olive oil on the side and served with soup, salad or pasta. Slice in half and fill with grilled vegetables for a gourmet sandwich. "

2 tsp	active dry yeast	¼ cup	rosemary, chopped
2 cups	warm water, 110°	2½ cups	whole wheat flour
¼ cup	honey	2½ cups	white bread flour
¼ cup	olive oil	1 cup	sundried tomatoes,
2 tsp	sea salt		chopped

Topping:

8 cloves	garlic, minced
¼ cup	olive oil
¼ cup	rosemary sprigs
	coarse sea salt
	fresh ground pepper

In a small bowl, mix the warm water with the honey, add the yeast and let stand 10 minutes until foamy.

In a large bowl combine the oil, salt, tomatoes and rosemary. Add the yeast and 1 cup of the whole wheat flour. Blend with a wooden spoon until well combined. Add the remaining whole wheat and the white flour, ½ cup at a time until you can turn the dough onto a floured work surface. Add any remaining flour while you knead. The dough should be soft and pliable but it will also feel a little sticky, add more flour if dough is wet.

Knead the dough for 5-10 minutes and then place in a lightly oiled bowl. Cover with a damp towel and let rise in a warm, draft free place for 1½ hours.

Punch the dough down. Lightly oil a large baking pan and turn the dough out onto the pan. Let it rest, covered with a tea towel for about 5 minutes.

Gently start stretching the dough to fill the pan. If you feel resistance leave the dough for a few minutes and then continue. Cover and let the dough rise again for 30 minutes.

In a small bowl mix the garlic with the olive oil. Make small indentations in the dough with your fingers and smear the olive oil mixture all over the dough. Sprinkle the dough with the rosemary, sea salt and fresh ground pepper.

Bake for 30 to 45 minutes in a preheated 350° oven until puffed and golden. Let cool for 5 minutes before cutting, if you can wait that long.

Sweet Potato Rosemary Foccacia Bread

Serves 12-15 (makes enough to fill a 15 x 10 inch pan)

Foccacia is great served with soup and salad, on its own, or as a base for sandwich fillings.

2½ tsp	active dry yeast	1 tbsp	sea salt
1 cup	warm water, 110°	¼ cup	olive oil
1 tbsp	honey	¼ cup	rosemary, chopped
2 cups	white bread flour	2 cups	sweet potatoes,
2½ cups	whole wheat flour		cooked and mashed

Topping:

1½ lbs	sweet potatoes, sliced thin
¼ cup	olive oil
2	garlic cloves minced
	extra rosemary for garnishing
	fresh ground pepper and coarse sea salt

In a small bowl, combine the yeast, water and honey and let stand for about 10 minutes until foamy. Add oil, salt and rosemary.

In a large bowl combine the white flour and about 2 cups of the whole wheat flour with the mashed sweet potatoes. It will be thick. Add the yeast and stir the dough until well combined.

Turn the dough onto a lightly floured surface and knead in remaining flour for about 10 minutes, it may be sticky and this is fine. Place dough in a lightly oiled bowl, cover and let rise in a warm place for 1½ hours.

In a saucepan with boiling salted water, blanch the potatoes for about 5 minutes. Remove from heat, strain and rinse with cold water. Put into a bowl with the remaining topping ingredients.

Punch the dough down and turn it out into a well oiled pan. Roll the dough out to fit the pan, cover and let rise again for about 45 minutes. Arrange the potatoes overlapping to cover the entire dough pan. Sprinkle with coarse salt and fresh pepper.

In a preheated 400° oven, bake the foccacia in the bottom third of the oven for about 40 minutes until golden and puffy. Let cool in the pan and serve warm or at room temperature.

Pita Bread ~ Three Ways

Makes about 2 dozen

Pita bread is so simple to make, the only tricky part comes in the baking. It may take a little practice but the end result is well worth the effort. You will need 2 large baking pans.

Basic Pita:

3 cups	warm water, 110°	2 tsp	sea salt
¼ cup	honey	2 cups	whole wheat flour
4 tsp	active dry yeast	3 cups	white bread flour
⅓ cup	olive oil		

Optional: add 2 tbsp each, sesame seeds, flax seeds and toasted millet, or add 2 tbsp toasted sesame seeds and ¼ cup minced onion

In a large bowl, dissolve honey in the warm water, add the yeast. Let stand for 15 minutes until foamy.

Add the olive oil, salt, whole wheat flour and optional ingredients if using, stirring well with a wooden spoon. Add the white flour and stir until it is firm enough to be moved to a work surface. Work in remaining flour and knead for about 5 minutes, the dough will be firm but soft. Place in a lightly oiled bowl covered with a damp cloth and let rise in a warm place for approximately 1½ hours. The dough should double in size.

Preheat the oven to 400°. Place baking sheets in the oven and do not remove until you are ready to bake the pitas. You should be able to fit about 4 large or 6 small pitas on them.

Punch down the dough, let rest for a couple of minutes before dividing into roughly 24 pieces. Using a rolling pin and a generous amount of flour, roll each piece of dough into a round about 5 inches in diameter and ½ inch thick. Place on the hot baking sheets and bake until each pita is puffed up and lightly browned, about 15 minutes.

Harmony Dawn Cornbread

Makes a 9 x 13 inch pan

This is a spicy, chunky cornbread that is packed with flavour. Serve with soup, salad, chili or just on its own as an afternoon snack.

¼ cup	unsalted butter, melted		1 cup	all-purpose flour
4	eggs, whisked		½ cup	whole wheat flour
1½ cups	buttermilk		1 tbsp	brown sugar
1½ tsp	puréed chipotle peppers		1 tbsp	baking powder
1½ cups	corn kernels, cooked		¾ tsp	baking soda
½ cup	cilantro, chopped fine		¼ tsp	sea salt
½ cup	roasted red pepper, minced		½ tsp	fresh ground pepper
1½ cups	fine cornmeal		1 cup	monterey jack cheese, grated

Preheat oven to 375°. Lightly butter baking dish.

In a large bowl combine all dry ingredients together, add cheese. In a separate bowl whisk together butter, eggs, buttermilk, chipotles. Add corn, cilantro and red pepper.

Pour over dry ingredients, stirring until just combined. Pour into baking dish and bake for 30 minutes or until golden brown.

> CHEF'S TIP:
>
> Chipotle peppers are sold in small cans in adobo sauce. Purée contents of the can and keep refrigerated for up to a month. You can roast your own red peppers but for a quick fix, purchase them jarred or at the deli counter in any supermarket.

Funky Rosemary Flatbread

Makes about 12

This is a fun bread, almost like a big warm cracker. You can keep it simple with just the herbs or for real "wow" factor, embellish with tomato and onion slices. Serve with dips, soups or on its own.

1½ tsp	active dry yeast	1 tsp	sea salt
3 cups	whole wheat flour + 2 tsp	2 tsp	ground pepper
1 tsp	honey	¼ cup	olive oil
1¼ cups	warm water, 110°	2 large	garlic cloves, minced
¼ cup	fine cornmeal	¼ fresh	rosemary leaves
1 tbsp	sundried tomatoes, minced	1 tbsp	black olives, minced

Optional Additions:

1	red onion, sliced very thin, lengthwise
12	cherry tomatoes, yellow, orange and red, sliced thinly
	whole sage, parsley, or rosemary leaves

I use my KitchenAid stand up mixer for this but you can do it by hand if you don't have one, it just takes longer.

In the bowl of the mixer, add ¼ cup of the warm water, mix in the honey and stir in the yeast. Let stand for 10 minutes until foamy.

In a separate bowl, mix together the remaining flour, cornmeal, rosemary, olives, tomatoes, salt and pepper. Add to the yeast mixture. On low speed, gradually add the remaining cup of water and mix until the dough just holds together. You may need to add a bit more water if necessary. Continue mixing about 5 minutes until you have a nice smooth elastic dough ball that is pulling away from the sides of the bowl.

Turn dough onto a lightly floured work surface and knead one minute or so.

Place dough in a lightly oiled bowl, cover and let rise in a warm place until doubled, approximately one hour. Return to floured surface and knead 10 times, cut into 12 equal balls, set aside.

Preheat oven to 400°. Working with one ball at a time, roll out to a 4 by 10 inch oval. Place on a parchment lined baking sheet. Combine olive oil and garlic together in a small bowl and brush flatbread. Sprinkle with coarse salt, freshly ground pepper and fresh herbs of choice and optional ingredients if using. Repeat with remaining flatbreads. Three to four will fit on one sheet, so you will have to work in batches. Bake 12 minutes or so until golden brown.

Sunflower Crackers

Makes about 50 crackers

" Homemade crackers have little in common with store bought crackers. You can cut them into any shape and the flavour and freshness is just out of this world. They keep for 2 weeks refrigerated in a sealed container, or freeze, wrapped well for up to 6 months. Bring to room temperature to serve. Substitute spelt or whole wheat flour if you like. "

5½ tbsp	sunflower seeds, toasted lightly and cooled
2 tbsp	pumpkin seeds, toasted lightly and cooled
1 cup	all-purpose flour
5½ tbsp	wheat germ
½ cup	rye flour
2 tsp	caraway seeds
5½ tbsp	extra virgin olive oil
	coarse sea salt to taste

In a food processor, grind the sunflower and pumpkin seeds with the flour, wheat germ, rye flour, and caraway seeds. With the motor running, add the oil and 6 tbsp of water and blend the mixture until it just forms a ball of dough.

Transfer the dough to a lightly floured surface and roll into an eighth of an inch thick square. Using a 1½ or 2 inch cookie cutter, cut the dough and transfer to an ungreased baking sheet.

Prick each square with a fork and sprinkle lightly with coarse salt. Bake in the middle of a preheated 400° oven for 10 to 12 minutes or until golden. Transfer the crackers to a cooling rack.

Cheddar Sesame Crisps

Makes about 50 crackers

These crisps are really fast and absolutely yummy. Serve with an antipasti platter or with pear chutney and a nice red wine for a great holiday appetizer. Substituting spelt or whole wheat flour for the white flour is fine. Crisps will keep for about two days in a tightly sealed container.

¼ lb	extra sharp white cheddar, grated
¼ lb	freshly grated Parmesan cheese
½ cup	cold, unsalted butter, cut into ½ inch bits
½ cup	whole wheat flour
½ cup	sesame seeds, toasted and cooled slightly
¼ cup	shallots, minced
½ tsp	sea salt
¼ tsp	dried chilies or more to taste
	white pepper to taste

Using a food processor, blend all ingredients until well combined and the mixture forms a ball of dough. Halve the dough, form into logs about 6 inches long and 1½ inches in diameter and chill, wrapped in plastic wrap for 1 to 2 hours or until firm enough to slice.

Cut the dough into ¼ inch slices, arrange the slices 2 inches apart on an ungreased baking sheet and bake in the middle of a preheated 400° oven for 5-7 minutes, or until the edges are golden brown. Transfer the crisps carefully to racks, let cool and then drain them on paper towels if desired.

Oatmeal Herb Crackers

Makes about 40 crackers

Excellent with dips, cheese, carrot pâté (pg.121), or just for snacking. Freeze in a tightly sealed container, bring to room temperature to serve.

2½ cups	rolled oats
2 tbsp	fresh dill
1 tbsp	fresh parsley
1 tbsp	sunflower oil
	coarse sea salt to taste
	pinch of white pepper

In a food processor, coarsely grind 1 cup of rolled oats. In a bowl, combine the ground oats with 1 cup of the remaining oats, dill, parsley and oil. Add ½ cup of water and stir the mixture until it forms into a dough.

Sprinkle ¼ cup of the remaining oats on a work surface and lay the dough on top. Pat the dough out slightly and sprinkle with the remaining ¼ cup oats.

Roll out the dough to ⅛ inch thick, and with a 2 inch round cookie cutter, cut out as many rounds as possible. Arrange on an ungreased baking sheet, prick with a fork and sprinkle with the coarse salt and white pepper.

Bake in the middle of a preheated 325° oven for 35 to 40 minutes or until they are golden. Transfer to racks and cool.

Mom's Pastry

Makes enough for 2 large pies

" This pastry is decadent, rich, flaky and a pure taste sensation. My mother Margaret is a fantastic baker and cook as was her mother, Gladys, and this is one of the gems that she has generously decided to share. "

The beauty of this pastry is that it is made in the food processor. The less your hands touch the pastry, the better. It freezes well, wrapped in foil and placed in a freezer bag. Defrost in the refrigerator.

2½ cups	all-purpose flour, whole wheat or spelt
1 tsp	organic cane sugar
1 tsp	sea salt
1 cup	chilled unsalted butter, cut into chunks
¼ cup	vegetable shortening or sunflower oil

Combine all ingredients together in a food processor except shortening/oil and blend until fine. Add shortening/oil and pulse once or twice. Trickle a third of a cup, chilled water gradually until mixture binds together but not in heavy clumps as it will be too wet. If you need more water add a tablespoon at a time.

Remove from food processor and shape into one or two rounds. Put mixture in foil or saran wrap and refrigerate for 1 hour or more. Remove, let rest for 15 minutes, then roll out pastry on a lightly floured surface.

Sweet Potato Cloverleaf Rolls

Makes 18 rolls

These rolls have a slightly sweet flavour from the potatoes. They are a soft roll, perfect for dinner. I have served them on any occasion but they seem especially suited to Thanksgiving or Christmas. Use spelt or whole wheat flour if you prefer but the texture will be heavier.

3 tbsp	honey
2½ tsp	active dry yeast
2	large eggs
⅓ cup	milk
¼ cup	unsalted butter, melted and cooled, plus 2 tbsp
1 tsp	sea salt
¾ cup	cooked sweet potatoes, or pumpkin, mashed
3½ cups	all-purpose flour

In a small bowl stir together 1 tbsp honey and ¼ cup of warm water, add yeast and let stand 10 minutes until foamy.

In a large bowl whisk together the eggs, the remaining 2 tbsp honey, milk, butter, salt, sweet potatoes, and the yeast mixture until well combined, stir in 3 cups of the flour, 1 cup at a time, and turn the dough onto a floured surface. Knead the dough, adding as much remaining flour as possible to form a smooth elastic dough.

Place dough in a lightly buttered bowl and cover with plastic wrap for 1 hour. Punch dough down, turn onto a floured surface, cut off pieces the size of walnuts and form into balls. Lightly butter 18 muffin tins and place 3 balls of dough into each, brushing with melted butter and let rise, loosely covered with wrap for 30 to 45 minutes. Bake in a preheated 400° oven for 12 to 15 minutes, until golden.

Black Olive Buckwheat Rolls

Makes 16 hearty rolls

These rolls have a Mediterranean flare and are quite hearty due to the buckwheat flour. They go well with stews and soups or "stinky pasta" (pg.158). I love making these in my KitchenAid which is a work horse, but you can blend by hand or with a food processor.

5 tsp	active dry yeast	3 cups	all-purpose flour
1 tsp	honey	1½ cups	kalamata olives,
1 tsp	freshly ground pepper		chopped
¾ cup	buckwheat flour	2 tbsp	olive oil

Optional:

2 tbsp	Italian parsley, minced
2 tbsp	garlic, minced

In bowl of KitchenAid, add yeast with 1 cup warm water, honey and pepper and let stand 10 minutes until foamy.

Add the buckwheat flour, all-purpose flour, olives, oil, optional additions and using the dough hook beat the mixture until it forms a soft, sticky dough. Knead the dough gently by hand on a floured surface for 2 minutes, dust it lightly with flour, and put in a lightly oiled bowl covered tightly with plastic wrap for 45 minutes to 1 hour until doubled in bulk.

Turn dough onto a floured surface and roll into a long log. Cut into equal sized pieces and form into dough balls. Arrange on a lightly oiled baking sheet, dusted with flour and let rise loosely covered, for 30 to 40 minutes.

Make a slash in the top about ¼ inch deep and bake in the lower third of a 400° oven for 20 to 25 minutes.

2

BREAKFAST BRUNCH & LUNCH

Maple Pecan Granola

Makes 15 cups

Pecans and maple syrup go together so well. Granola will keep for about two weeks in an airtight container.

10 cups	organic oats		½ cup	sunflower oil
2 cups	sunflower seeds		½ cup	maple syrup
½ cup	flax seeds		1½ cups	Thompson raisins
2 cups	pecans, coarsely chopped			
2 tsp	cinnamon			
¼ tsp	ground cloves			

Preheat oven to 300°. Have ready 2 large baking sheets.

In a large bowl combine the oats, seeds, nuts and spices.

In a small bowl mix together the oil, maple syrup and vanilla.

Pour liquid ingredients over dry ingredients and mix thoroughly. Spread the granola on the baking sheets and bake for about 45 minutes, checking and turning every 15 minutes to ensure even baking. Granola is done when it is a nice golden brown.

Return to bowl, add raisins, mixing thoroughly. Let cool and store accordingly.

Honey Almond Granola

Makes 15 cups

10 cups	organic oats		⅔ cup	sunflower oil
2 cups	sunflower seeds		⅔ cup	honey
½ cup	unhulled sesame seeds		1 tsp	pure vanilla extract
2 cups	almonds, coarsely chopped		1 tsp	almond extract
2 tsp	cinnamon		1½ cups	sultanas
1 tsp	grated fresh nutmeg			

Optional Additions:

1 cup	dried cranberries
½ cup	dried blueberries

Preheat oven to 300°. Have ready 2 large baking pans.

Combine all dry ingredients together in a large bowl.

In a small sauce pan, heat the liquid ingredients over medium heat, approximately 2 minutes, until the honey becomes runny.

Combine liquid and dry ingredients together until well mixed. Divide evenly among pans and bake for about 45 minutes, turning every 15 minutes until golden brown.

Remove from oven, return to bowl, add sultanas and any optional additions.

Harmony Dawn French Toast

Serves 2-4

Serve with any of the fruit embellishments (pg.38) topped with maple syrup. Garnish with pansies or other edible flowers. Substitute your favourite bread for the whole wheat. You will need about 2 slices per person.

1 loaf	whole wheat bread, crusts removed, cut into thick 1 inch slices
4	eggs
½ cup	cream or soy milk
½ tsp	freshly grated nutmeg
½ tsp	cinnamon
1½ tsp	or more, freshly grated, organic orange zest
Pinch	sea salt
1 tbsp	unsalted butter

In a large bowl whisk the eggs, spices and orange zest. Soak the bread slices in the egg mixture until drenched, dripping off excess. Either bake or fry bread, turning once until golden brown. Slice in half, on the diagonal and serve immediately with a dusting of organic, powdered white sugar.

CHEF'S TIP:

To bake, heat a buttered cookie sheet in a 350° oven for 5 minutes. Place bread on pan and bake for about 10 minutes per side, using more butter if sticky.

To fry, heat butter over medium heat until melted, add bread and cook about 4 minutes per side until brown and crispy.

Oatmeal Porridge

Serves 4

Serve with warm apple preserves (pg.39), warm soy or rice milk, and maple syrup. Sprinkle with toasted coconut, walnuts or pecans. Substitute cow's milk for the soy milk if desired.

1½ cups	organic quick cooking oats
¾ tsp	sea salt
2½ cups	water
½ cup	soy or rice milk
½ tsp	vanilla extract
½ tsp	freshly grated nutmeg
½ tsp	cinnamon

Put oats, salt and water in a sauce pan and bring to a boil. Reduce heat, add soy or rice milk, vanilla and spices and simmer on low, stirring until creamy, about 3-5 minutes. Remove from heat and let sit a few minutes before serving.

Fruit Embellishments

Fruit embellishments are multi-purpose, you can use them as toppings for french toast, granola or porridge. However, they are just as good over ice cream or as a filling for dessert crêpes.

Buttered Pears

Serves 2

2 tbsp	unsalted butter	2 tbsp	maple syrup
½ tsp	cinnamon	2 tbsp	brandy or Poire William,
3	Bartlett pears, peeled,		or to taste
	sliced into eights		

In a skillet over medium low heat, melt the butter and add pears. Cook about 2 minutes until heated through and the pears are soft but not wet. Add cinnamon, maple sugar and liquor, if using. Toss to cover and serve immediately.

Berry Fruit Compotes

Serves 2

Into a large pot over medium heat add:

2 cups	strawberries, blueberries, raspberries or blackberries
Add	one peeled & sliced peach, pear or apple

Bring to a boil, turn down heat and simmer gently for up to 10 minutes, trying to keep compote as chunky as possible. Add ½ tsp lemon, lime or orange zest depending on preference. Taste. If you think it needs a little sweetness then add 1 tbsp of maple syrup. Serve warm or at room temperature.

Fried Bananas with Sultanas

Serves 2

If you are in the mood for extravagance here you go!

3	bananas cut into ½ inch slices
½ cup	sultanas
¼ cup	unsalted butter
½ tsp	mace

In a skillet over medium heat, melt butter, add mace. Toss in bananas and cook until slightly caramelized, about 5-8 minutes. Add sultanas and serve warm.

Warm Apple Preserves

Serves 4

4-6	organic apples, peeled, cored and sliced into eights
2 tbsp	lemon juice
2 tbsp	water

Optional: ½ tsp cinnamon and ½ tsp nutmeg or
½ tsp anise, ½ tsp orange zest, ½ cup fresh cranberries

In a large saucepan over medium low heat, cook apples, lemon and water until apples have lost their shape slightly. Add any optional items if desired, and serve warm.

Black Rice Congee with Ginger Sauce

Serves 4

Congee is a creamy rice porridge and there are as many versions by as many different nations across the globe. I have included two in my book, one savoury and one sweet, both satisfying in their own way.

Black rice is slightly sweet, glutinous and has a real woodsy flavour and aroma. Serve this congee with condiments like Furitake, a prepared sesame and seaweed mixture or Nanami Togarashi, assorted chili peppers with orange and seaweed. Both are available at Japanese or Asian stores. The ginger sauce is one of Andy's famous concoctions.

4 dried	shiitake mushrooms	2 tbsp	tamari
4 cups	cooked, black rice	2 tbsp	fresh ginger, peeled and cut into ¼ inch circles

Put shiitakes in a small saucepan and cover with water. Bring to a boil, simmer for 15 minutes, remove from heat and let sit 15 minutes. Drain, reserving cooking water and coarsely chop.

In a large pot over medium low heat, add the rice, ginger, shiitakes, tamari and about 2 cups of water to cover, plus shiitake water. Simmer until rice is creamy, stirring frequently. You may need to add more water.

Ginger Sauce

2 inch	piece of ginger, peeled & chopped
3 tbsp	toasted sesame oil
¼ cup	tamari

In a saucepan over medium high heat, cook the ginger in the sesame oil until brown and crispy. Pour into a bowl, add tamari, stir and serve by the teaspoon over the congee.

Coconut Cardamom Brown Rice Congee

Serves 4-6

This is a lovely, creamy, sweet congee. This is great for breakfast or served as a dessert, similar to rice pudding. Serve with sliced bananas and diced mangoes.

4 cups	cooked, brown rice
2 cans	coconut milk
½ cup	honey or brown sugar
1 tsp	cardamom
1 tsp	cinnamon
2 cups	raisins
1 cup	toasted almond slivers

In a large pot over medium low heat, cook all the ingredients except the almonds, until a gruel like consistency is achieved. You may need to add a little water, stirring frequently for approximately 40 minutes. Add almonds and adjust seasonings.

Mango Berry Swiss Muesli

Serves 4

> "Swiss muesli is made with oats that have generally been soaked in cream or yoghurt, with fresh fruit and nuts added. Mine is a combination of everything, with fruit being the star performer. The beauty of muesli is that you make it the night before and let it sit in the fridge overnight. Substitute soy or rice milk for the cream. Any combination of fresh fruit can be used but in a pinch use good quality frozen fruit."

4 cups	organic quick oats
1 large	container, organic strawberry yoghurt
1 cup	cream or cranberry juice
2 large	mangoes, peeled, pitted and diced
2 pints	fresh organic strawberries, chopped
1 pint	wild blueberries
1 cup	dried cranberries, optional
1 cup	Thompson raisins, optional
1 cup	toasted almond slivers

In a large bowl that will fit into the fridge, mix all ingredients together except almonds. Stir until well combined. Place in the fridge and leave overnight. In the morning, stir, adding more yoghurt or juice if necessary to produce a nice smooth consistency. Bring to room temperature, stir in almonds and serve.

Potato Chickpea and Arugula Frittata

Serves 8

This is a wonderful dish and very satisfying. If you would like a fish alternative, substitute 1 cup smoked salmon for the chickpeas and ¼ cup fresh dill instead of the parsley.

2 tbsp	olive oil		¼ tsp	dried chilies
1 tbsp	unsalted butter		2 cups	fresh baby arugula
2½ cups	gold potatoes, diced		8	eggs
½ cup	minced green onions		½ cup	cream
1	roasted yellow pepper		½ cup	Italian parsley, chopped
1 cup	cooked chickpeas			sea salt and fresh pepper

Preheat oven to broil.

In a stove to oven skillet, over medium heat, cook the potatoes and onions in the olive oil and butter until potatoes are soft, approximately 8 minutes. Add chopped yellow pepper, chick peas, chilies and ½ tsp salt. Cook for about a minute. Add arugula and cook another minute.

Meanwhile, whisk eggs with cream, parsley and ground pepper to taste. Add egg mixture to pan and cook about 2 minutes or until set. Put in oven and cook about 8 minutes until puffy, set and golden brown. The edges will be pulling away from the sides. Remove from oven and let sit 5 minutes.

Sprinkle top of frittata with chopped cherry or orange tomatoes and serve sliced, into wedges.

Basic Crêpe Recipe

Makes approximately 12 crêpes

The beauty of crêpes is they can be made ahead of time and refrigerated or frozen until ready to use. You can put just about any filling in them that you like; lemon juice and zest with powdered sugar or fresh wild blueberries and cream, fruit compote or buttered pears. They can also be savoury; brie and asparagus or roasted mushrooms and cheese. They taste fantastic simply served on their own with maple syrup like a light pancake.

Crêpe batter should sit refrigerated for a couple of hours or overnight to give flour time to absorb the liquid.

1½ cups	milk
⅔ cup	all-purpose flour, spelt or whole wheat
½ tsp	sea salt
3	eggs
	unsalted, melted butter

In a medium bowl, whisk 2 tbsp melted butter with remaining ingredients. Cover and refrigerate.

Brush bottom of crêpe pan with melted butter over medium high heat. Pour or ladle ¼ cup batter in pan and swirl to coat bottom. Cook until set. Using a spatula, lift edge and flip over to the other side. Cook until golden. Remove from pan and place stacked on a sheet of parchment or waxed paper.

Asparagus and Brie Crêpes with Dill

Serves 6

Basic Crêpe Recipe

1 large	bunch, Ontario asparagus, ends trimmed
½ tsp	sea salt
1 small	package of brie cut into slices, about 8 ounces
1 tsp	lemon zest grated
	dill and chive sprigs
	ice water bath

Have ready 6 to 8 warm crêpes. Preheat the oven to 250°.

In a large pot of boiling, salted water, cook the asparagus for about 5 minutes. Remove and drop into the ice water bath. Drain, place asparagus on a towel to remove excess water, set aside.

Working with one crêpe at a time, place 3 spears of asparagus on the crêpe so the heads will slightly stick out one end. Add a couple of pieces of brie length wise on the asparagus, dill and chive sprigs and a grate of lemon zest.

Roll the crêpe so you have a nice envelope and place on a warm baking tray in the oven. Proceed with the rest. Serve on a platter garnished with extra herbs and fresh nasturtium flowers.

Swiss Cheese and Onion Quiche

Makes a 9 inch pie and serves 6

" I include this recipe because it is one of Andy's favourites. It is extremely versatile, serve it for brunch, dinner or for breakfast. Pair it with a simple salad and crusty brown bread and you have a complete meal. "

Pastry for one 9 inch pie (pg.29)		1 cup	half & half cream
2 tbsp	unsalted butter	3	eggs, whisked
1	vidalia onion, chopped	1 tsp	sea salt
1 tbsp	all-purpose flour		freshly ground pepper
2 cups	swiss cheese, grated		thin tomato slices for garnish

Preheat oven to 400°.

Roll the pastry out on a lightly floured surface. Fit over pie plate, trim edges.

In a small skillet over medium heat, cook onion in the butter until tender, about 5 minutes. Spread evenly around the pie crust base. In a small bowl, toss the flour with the cheese and sprinkle over onions.

In a bowl, whisk together cream, eggs and salt. Pour over the cheese and generously grind pepper over the top. If desired place the tomato slices decoratively over the top of the quiche.

Bake 10 minutes. Turn oven down to 325° and bake another 30 to 35 minutes until golden brown and puffy. Let pie sit for 10 minutes then cut into wedges.

Zucchini & Sundried Tomato Frittata

Serves 8

This is a wonderful satisfying dish that can be served for breakfast, lunch or dinner. Serve with fresh baguette, salad and fresh tomato, basil salsa. Add sliced zucchini flowers to the mix for an interesting addition.

2 tbsp	olive oil		½ cup	sundried tomatoes
1 tbsp	unsalted butter		8	eggs, whisked
2 cups	zucchini, chopped		½ cup	chopped Italian parsley
6	green onions, diced		½ tsp	sea salt
2 cups	swiss chard, shredded			freshly ground pepper
½ cup	grated Parmesan cheese		1 tsp	chipotle purée, optional

Preheat oven to broil.

In a large stove to oven skillet and over medium high heat, add the oil and butter, making sure all the sides of pan are oiled. Add zucchini and green onions, cook about 3 minutes until just tender. Add the swiss chard and zucchini flowers, (if available), cooking until the chard is soft but not wet. Add the chopped sundried tomatoes, making sure the vegetables are spread evenly around the pan.

While the vegetables are cooking, whisk eggs with the parsley, salt and pepper.

Add eggs to pan and cook for about 2 minutes until the eggs are slightly set. Remove from heat, sprinkle with cheese and put in the oven on the top shelf about 4 inches from the heat. Cook about 10 minutes until puffy and the sides have pulled away from the pan.

Allow the frittata to sit about 5 minutes until set and then slice into sections. Can be served hot or at room temperature.

Leek, Mushroom and Brie Torta

Serves 8-12 depending on serving size

This is a really easy, make ahead dish that is rich and yummy and will serve a large group of people. Substitute smoked salmon for the mushrooms for a non vegetarian version. Serve with a light salad and tomato slices.

1 tbsp	olive oil	1 cup	cheddar cheese, grated
1 tbsp	unsalted butter		
6	leeks, white part, chopped	8 oz	Brie, chopped
1 tsp	dried thyme	1½ tbsp	dijon mustard
2 cups	mushrooms, sliced	1 tsp	tobasco
12	slices of multi-grain bread, crusts removed	6	eggs, beaten
		3 cups	half and half cream
			sea salt and pepper

Heat oil/butter in a skillet over medium heat. Add leeks and cook for about 3 minutes until they start to soften. Add thyme, mushrooms, salt and pepper, and cook until mushrooms are golden. Remove from heat.

Butter a 9 x 13 baking dish. Layer half of the bread slices. Top with half of the vegetable mixture followed by half of the brie and cheddar. Make a second layer of bread, vegetables and cheese.

Whisk together the remaining ingredients, adding a ¼ tsp of salt and pepper. Pour over the bread layers. Cover and let sit for one hour or overnight in the refrigerator. Bring to room temperature before baking.

Preheat oven to 350° and bake for 40 minutes or until puffed and set. Cool for 5 minutes before serving.

Summary Tomato Tart

Serves 4-6

Think of this as a twist on bruschetta. Light, crunchy and lovely served for lunch or as a funky summer canapé.

1 pkg	frozen puff pastry
3-4	fresh tomatoes, sliced thinly
1	small red onion, cut into slivers
2	garlic cloves, minced
2 tbsp	olive oil
¼ cup	each basil and Italian parsley, chopped
½ cup	grated fresh Parmesan

Preheat oven to 350°.

Defrost the pastry according to package directions. Roll out pastry on a lightly floured surface to make a thin rectangle, approximately 10 inches long by 8 inches wide. Fold the edge over and press, making a crust.

In a small bowl, mix the oil with the garlic and brush over the bottom and the edges of the tart. Sprinkle with the Parmesan, salt, pepper and onion slivers. Arrange the tomato slices, overlapping to cover the entire tart. Sprinkle with the fresh herbs, Parmesan and another grind of pepper.

Bake for approximately 20 to 25 minutes until golden brown and crunchy. Cut into large squares and serve.

Potato Pesto Pizza

Makes a 15 inch round pizza or an 11 x 15 rectangle

" Homemade pizza is in a class all its own. Everyone loves pizza, the fun that goes into the preparation, and the aromas from baking. Preparation is even easier if you make the dough in advance and freeze it. Defrost in the refrigerator overnight and bring to room temperature and proceed. You can purchase ready made pesto sauce or make your own. "

Pizza Dough Recipe (pg. 15)

¾ cup	pesto sauce	2 tbsp	olive oil
3 cups	thinly sliced potatoes	1 cup	swiss chard, chopped
3 large	garlic cloves minced	3 tbsp	fresh rosemary chopped
½ cup	chopped black olives	Juice	of half a lemon
1½ cups	feta, crumbled	½ cup	sundried tomatoes, chopped
1½ cups	mozzarella cheese, grated		sea salt & fresh pepper

Prepare the pizza dough. While the dough is rising prepare the potatoes. Preheat oven to 375°. In a large bowl combine potatoes, garlic, rosemary, lemon, salt, pepper and olive oil. Spread on a large baking sheet and roast 25 minutes until golden brown, set aside.

Turn oven up to 450°. Punch the dough down. Let rest a minute or two. Using a pizza pan or an oiled baking sheet, stretch the dough to fit the pan. If you feel resistance, leave for a minute or two and resume; remember to be kind to it.

Spread the bottom of the crust with pesto sauce, sprinkle with mozzarella. Layer remaining ingredients followed by feta and mozzarella. Turn oven down to 375° and bake on the bottom rack for 20 minutes or until the crust is golden and the cheese is melted.

Harmony Dawn Margarita Pizza

Makes a 15 inch round pizza or an 11 x 15 rectangle

A simple twist on a standard pizza. Roasting the cherry tomatoes caramelizes them and brings out their natural sweetness. Use homemade or store bought tomato sauce.

Pizza Dough Recipe (pg. 15)

1 pint	cherry tomatoes, sliced in half
1 cup	tomato sauce, approximately
1	bunch fresh basil, leaves left whole
2 tbsp	garlic, minced
1 cup	mozzarella
½ cup	freshly grated Parmesan
	sea salt and pepper

Preheat oven to 350°. Place tomatoes, cut side up, on an oiled baking sheet and sprinkle with a little salt. Roast for 25 minutes. Remove from oven and set aside.

Turn oven up to 450°. Punch the dough down. Let rest a minute or two. Using a pizza pan or an oiled baking sheet, stretch the dough to fit the pan. If you feel resistance, leave for a minute or two and resume.

Spread a thin layer of tomato sauce over the dough and sprinkle the garlic randomly over the pizza. Sprinkle the Parmesan and then place the tomatoes, cut side up, the basil leaves and finally the mozzarella. Grind a bit of pepper over the pizza.

Turn oven down to 375° and bake in the bottom of the oven for 20 minutes until golden and cheese has melted.

Roasted Root Vegetable Quesadillas

Serves 4-6

" This is a creation by my dear friend and chef, Moira Nordholt, who is one of our biggest supporters. She made these in the early days of Harmony Dawn and since then I have tailored them with my own spin. I make them all the time because they are so tasty, and also because it fills me with nostalgia for my friend, who now lives far away. "

6	different colored wraps; flax, spinach, whole grain, tomato
5 cups	mixed vegetables; parsnips, carrots, squash, yams, beets, peeled and sliced thinly
1	red onion, sliced thinly
2 cups	monterey jack cheese, grated
1 cup	old cheddar cheese, grated
	olive oil, sea salt & ground pepper

Preheat oven to 350°.

In a large bowl, toss the vegetables with olive oil, salt and pepper to cover, and place in a single layer on a baking sheet or two. Bake for 25 to 40 minutes turning every 10 minutes until golden and cooked. Put back in the bowl when cooked.

Lay the wraps on the work surface and place about ¾ of a cup of vegetables on one half of each wrap, sprinkle generously with both cheeses. Fold in half, place on a baking sheet and bake for 5 to 7 minutes per side. Remove and cut into triangles. Serve with avocado salad (pg.71) or any other bean dip.

Mushroom Gruyère Quesadillas

Serves 4

I got the inspiration for this recipe when Andy and I visited a lovely crêperie in Quebec City. It was a wonderful combination and taste sensation, so I retrofit the ingredients in a quesadilla. Enjoy!

4	wraps, flax or whole wheat
4 to 5	portobello mushrooms cut into ¼ inch slices
1	orange bell pepper
1½ cups	gruyère cheese, use swiss if unobtainable
¾ cup	feta cheese
	olive oil, sea salt & ground pepper

There are two ways of roasting the vegetables for this recipe. Either use a stove top grill pan or roast in the oven, it will depend on how many you are making. I have used the oven for this recipe.

Turn oven to broil. Oil a baking sheet and place the mushrooms and pepper in a single layer, brush with oil and sprinkle with salt and pepper. Cook about 5 minutes and turn over, cooking until the mushrooms begin to release their juice. Remove and place in a bowl to let excess moisture drip off. Turn oven down to 350°.

Lay the wraps on your work surface and place a few mushrooms and peppers on one half. Sprinkle generously with gruyère and a touch of feta. Repeat with remaining wraps. Fold in half, place on baking sheet and bake for 5 minutes turning once and baking on the other side until crisp. Cut into triangles and serve.

Tapas ~ Grilled Tarragon Asparagus

Serves 4

Serve the asparagus as part of a tapas platter. Tapas are a selection of small dishes that compliment each other. Served on festive platters, they are casual yet have a gourmet flare. More importantly, they taste out of this world. Serve with crusty garlic bread or bruschetta and of course, sangria.

¾ lb	Ontario spring asparagus
1 tbsp	white wine vinegar
1 tsp	dijon mustard
1 tsp	dried tarragon or 1 tbsp fresh
½ tsp	sea salt
¼ tsp	freshly ground pepper
3 tbsp	olive oil

Trim about an inch off the bottom of the asparagus and place in a bowl. In a small bowl whisk together remaining ingredients. Pour over asparagus, marinate for 30 minutes.

Preheat BBQ and grill asparagus, reserving marinade, for about 5 minutes until crisp tender. Serve with remaining marinade. Alternatively roast in a pan in the oven with the marinating sauce.

Tapas ~ Tofu or Shrimp in Spicy Garlic

Serves 4

Juicy shrimp or tofu go together so well with the chilies and paprika. Fast and versatile either as a main dish for 2 or as part of a tapas platter.

1 pkg	extra firm tofu cut into ½ inch chunks or
¾ lb	large shrimp, peeled
3 tbsp	olive oil
3-4	cloves of garlic, minced
¼ tsp	dried chilies
1 tsp	sherry vinegar
2 tbsp	chopped parsley
½ tsp	Spanish paprika

In a heavy skillet, heat the oil over medium heat until very hot. Add the shrimp or tofu in a single layer and sprinkle with the garlic and pepper flakes.

Cook for about 2 minutes and then flip to cook other side, until shrimp are pink or the tofu is cooked through. Stir in the vinegar, parsley and paprika and serve immediately.

Tapas ~ Baguette with Wild Mushroom Sauce

Serves 4-8 depending on serving size

Serve as part of a tapas platter or simply on its own for a quick lunch. Any combination of mushrooms is delicious; shiitakes, portobellos, chanterelles or morels.

1½ lbs	wild mushrooms, any combination
2 tbsp	olive oil
1 tbsp	unsalted butter
4	garlic cloves, minced
2 tbsp	Italian parsley, minced
½ tsp	Spanish paprika
¼ tsp	dried chilies
	sea salt & freshly ground pepper
	slices of smoky gruyère cheese - optional
	baguette cut into large slices

Clean mushrooms with a damp cloth. Try not to get the gills too wet or dish will be soggy. Remove ends and slice mushrooms.

In a large skillet, over medium heat, cook the mushrooms and garlic in the oil and butter. Sprinkle with salt and pepper and cook until golden, about 8 minutes. Sprinkle with parsley, paprika and dried chilies.

Preheat broiler. Brush baguette with a little olive oil and broil for 1 to 2 minutes until slightly crisp. Top with mushroom mixture and a slice of cheese if using and broil until melted. Serve immediately.

Tapas ~ Potato Tortilla

Serves 6-8

A simple, satisfying dish that can be made ahead of time and served hot or at room temperature. Cut into pie shapes or small squares and serve as a cocktail appetizer. The chipotle peppers will add a smoky flavour to the dish.

½ cup	olive oil		6	eggs
2	garlic cloves, minced		1 tsp	chipotle pepper purée
1 large	Spanish onion, sliced thinly		2	spring onions, minced
4 large	Yukon gold potatoes, peeled and thinly sliced			sea salt & fresh pepper

In a large pot of boiling salted water, cook potatoes for 5 minutes. Remove and rinse under cold water. Pat dry.

Heat ¼ cup of oil in a large skillet over medium heat until hot. Sprinkle the potato slices with salt and pepper and fry until golden. You may need to cook two batches. Line a plate with a thick paper towel and transfer cooked potatoes to the plate to drain.

When all the potatoes are done, cook onion and garlic in remaining oil over medium to low heat for about 15 minutes until they are golden. Layer the potato slices on top and remove from heat.

In a bowl, whisk together the eggs, chipotles, a pinch of salt and freshly ground pepper. Pour over the potatoes and return the skillet to medium heat. Cook, shaking the pan to prevent sticking until the sides are set, about 4 minutes. Preheat broiler and broil tortilla about 5 minutes until completely set.

Run a knife around sides to release. Invert a plate over top and flip upside down to turn out tortilla. Sprinkle with spring onions and cut into cubes or wedges.

Harmony Dawn Brown Rice Sushi

Serves 4

Our version of vegetable sushi adds a macrobiotic twist. The addition of tahini creates an alkaline dish and adding tamari makes it savoury and satisfying.

Exact measurements are not that important in this recipe, just play, taste and have fun. Serve with condiments such as tamari, wasabi and pickled ginger with a side sea vegetable salad (pg.82). You will need a bamboo sushi rolling mat, available at Asian markets.

3 cups	cooked organic brown rice	½ an avocado, sliced thinly
¼ cup	tahini	julienned carrot & red pepper
1 tbsp	tamari	¼ of a cucumber, julienned
½ tsp	mirin	salad greens
4	toasted nori sheets	sprouts
5	shiitake mushrooms, cooked, sliced thinly	toasted sesame seeds

In a large bowl mix together the rice, tahini, tamari and mirin until well blended. Taste and adjust seasonings by adding more tahini or tamari. It shouldn't be too wet.

Working with one nori sheet at a time, lay shiny side down on your bamboo mat. Spread a handful of rice in the centre of the nori and press down making a 3 inch strip and leaving a 1 inch band closest to you. Pat down and make a slight groove down the centre of the roll.

In this groove place your avocado, carrots, red pepper, cucumber, shiitakes, whatever you choose but don't make it too thick. Sprinkle with sesame seeds.

Roll the mat, starting from the front edge and rolling away from you, so that the rice and filling are enclosed in the nori. Dampen the edge of the nori to help it stick. Remove the rolled sushi from the mat and place joint side down. Set aside and continue with the rest.

Using a sharp knife dipped in hot water, trim and discard the ends, then cut the roll into 1 inch thick pieces. The sushi can be made in advance, left whole, wrapped in plastic and left in a cool place until serving.

CHEF'S TIP:

Nori sheets come pre-toasted or plain. You can toast them yourself by carefully holding over a gas flame for a couple of seconds, until crisp. An electric element will work as well.

Vegetable Extravaganza Wraps

Makes 8 half wraps

" You can put anything your heart desires in a wrap to make it fun, tasty and nutritious. I have no guidelines when preparing, other than what I have on hand at the time. Sometimes a sauce I have made will be the inspiration or having an over abundance of rice or avocado. You are only limited by your imagination. Trust. "

Try to use a combination of colourful wraps if serving on a platter for a group. For the base, use any of the following; hummus, roasted red pepper sauce, black bean hummus, zesty beet sauce. Take your pick, they all add their own flair to the final product. If time permits make your own wraps from scratch, it is really easy to do, however store bought are a fine substitute. Serve these wraps with a side of Avocado Salad (pg.71), or any of the above mentioned sauces, fresh crudités and green salad.

4	wraps of your choice, spinach, tomato, flax, or whole grain
2	beets, grated with excess juice squeezed out
3	carrots, grated
1	yellow bell pepper, julienned
2	avocados, peeled and cut into ½ inch strips
	mixed organic greens
	alfalfa sprouts, broccoli sprouts or spicy radish sprouts

Lay the wraps out on the counter. Spread your choice of sauce as a base over wrap, leaving 1 inch around the edge.

Start layering the vegetables beginning with the beets and ending with the sprouts. Roll tightly, turning ends in while rolling to create a pocket, cut in half on the diagonal.

African Wraps

Makes 8 half wraps

I love peanuts and I love yams. They seem to go together beautifully, whether it be in a soup, stew or roasted with a peanut satay. These wraps are high in antioxidants, protein and beta carotene. Serve with a green salad and tahini sesame dressing (pg.102).

4	wraps, preferably whole wheat or flax
3 cups	cooked, organic short grain brown rice
¾ cup	crunchy peanut butter
1 tsp	tamari
3 cups	yams, cut into wedges
2 tsp	sesame oil
1 tsp	unhulled sesame seeds
1	bunch kale
½ cup	toasted, unsalted peanuts, chopped
	sea salt & pepper to taste

Optional: ¾ tsp dried chiles or 1 tsp of tobasco sauce

Preheat oven to 350°. Mix the yams with the sesame oil, sprinkle with the sesame seeds and roast for approximately 30 minutes, until tender yet crispy on the outside. Remove hard stems from kale and steam until bright green. Lay on a towel and pat dry. Set aside.

Combine the peanut butter, tamari, chilies and brown rice, sprinkle with salt and pepper.

To assemble, lay all the wraps on the counter. Place equal amounts of rice mixture on half of each wrap, leaving 1 inch from edge. Sprinkle with peanuts, then layer yams and kale and roll tightly. Dab a small amount of peanut butter along edge to help stick. Slice in half.

Gary's Allergy Wrap

Makes 8 half wraps

> "Named after Gary, a lovely man with so many food allergies. Through the process of elimination and what I had on hand, I came up with these. They were a hit with everyone in the group, and Gary requested that they be in my book. I have found that inspiration comes when you least expect it and usually out of tight situations."

4	wraps, spinach or whole wheat
3 cups	cooked black sweet rice, approximately
2 large	avocados, peeled and seeded
2 tsp	Braggs
1 tsp	lemon juice
¾ cup	unsalted cashews, roasted
2 cups	butternut squash cut into ¾ inch wedges
2 cups	sweet potato cut into ¾ inch wedges
2 tbsp	olive oil
	handful of salad greens
	sea salt & fresh pepper

Preheat oven to 350°. In a bowl toss the squash and sweet potato with the olive oil, sprinkle with salt and pepper. Roast in oven for approximately 30 minutes or until tender.

In a small bowl, mash the avocados with a fork and sprinkle with the lemon juice and Braggs. Grind the cashews in a blender or food processor until medium ground. Add to avocados and blend until smooth. Add salt and pepper to taste.

To assemble, lay all wraps on counter. Place a small amount of avocado mixture on the wrap leaving a 1 inch space from the edge in.

Place approximately ¾ cup black rice on one half side of the wrap, making sure it is about ¼ of an inch thick. Add a couple of the squash and sweet potato wedges to cover the length of the wrap, season with salt and pepper and throw in a handful of greens.

Roll tightly and cut on a diagonal. The avocado will secure the wrap.

Curried Chick Peas

Serves 2

This is so simple and super fast. Serve over brown basmati rice with a side of garlic pitas and salad greens for a nutritious meal. Use medium hot, or extra hot curry paste depending on your preference.

1	medium onion, sliced into slivers
1 can	chick peas drained, rinsed and dried ~19 oz
¼ cup	hot curry paste, Madras brand if possible
2 tsp	lemon juice
½	small pkg, fresh baby spinach, about 2 cups
1 tbsp	olive oil
2	plum tomatoes, diced

In a skillet over medium heat, fry the onions in the oil until golden, approximately 5 minutes. Add chick peas and sauté until chick peas are slightly browned. Lower heat, add the curry paste and lemon juice, blending thoroughly.

Add spinach, cover allowing steam to cook spinach about 1 minute. Uncover and mix spinach into chick peas. Add the diced tomatoes and serve.

Sautéed Spicy Salmon

Serves 2

This is the epitome of fast food in my book, except it is much better for you. Serve stuffed into a warm pita with a side green salad for a nutritious lunch, or serve with roasted rosemary potatoes (pg.92) and steamed vegetables for a quick mid week comfort menu.

1 can	wild sockeye salmon, crumbled
1	small yellow onion, sliced into slivers
¼ tsp	dried chilies
½ tbsp	olive oil
	sea salt & pepper to taste

Heat oil in a small frying pan. Add onions and fry until golden and crunchy. Add salmon, chilies, salt and pepper and heat until cooked through. The salmon will become pinkish in colour. Serve.

CHEF'S TIP:

Condiments such as homemade ketchup or chipotle mayonnaise are really good with the salmon and lend a fast food flare, which is especially enticing to children.

3

SALADS & SALAD DRESSING

Great Greens ~ Cold

When I put together a green salad it is usually to accompany a main dish of some sort, whether it is soup, burgers, pot pie, or quesadillas, they go with pretty much anything. I use only organic greens and they are available now in abundance at most supermarkets and of course health food stores. During the summer I grow them myself in my garden.

The best greens to use are combination packages. Select packages that contain a mixture of arugula, beet, mustard, buttercrunch and red lettuces. These offer a lot of different flavours, with each green providing different nutrients.

The base of the green salad is simply to throw fresh cleaned greens of choice into a big bowl. Next, the accompanying vegetables are to go on top, which usually depends on what is being served with the salad. For example, if the main dish is Asian oriented, I use daikon, jicama, red radishes and onion sprouts and arrange them decoratively throughout the salad.

I refrain from adding salad dressings as I have found most people prefer to add these themselves and the greens look so attractive in their natural raw state.

The one item I never put on my green salads are tomatoes. They make the salad soggy and unappealing. I prefer to put them on the side garnished with fresh herbs. They themselves are a star attraction.

Salad additions can be any combination of the following, sliced any way that suits your fancy, julienned, diagonally, grated or chunky. Choose from each category to build a great salad or just mix and match.

1. Broccoli sprouts, radish sprouts, spicy onion sprouts, mung bean sprouts.

2. Green, red, yellow or orange peppers, julienned.

3. Purple cabbage, green cabbage, bok choy, daikon, thinly sliced.

4. Fresh herbs, basil, parsley, mint, summer savoury, marjoram, lemon balm.

5. Toasted pumpkin, sunflower, sesame or millet seeds.

6. Grated carrots, beets or zucchini.

7. Apple, pear, or jicama sliced thinly.

8. Toasted walnuts, almonds or pecans, coarsely chopped.

9. Edible flowers, calendula, pansies, johnny jump ups, hollyhock, nasturtiums, basil flowers, oregano flowers.

Bold Hot Greens

Hot greens are a real treat. Easy to prepare, they can stand alone as a salad or accompany tofu steaks, curries, pot pies; the list only ends when your imagination does.

The method I use is very simple. Start with a wok or a large deep pan, add about ¼ cup of water and turn the heat to high. When the water is boiling rapidly add the greens. Cover for 1 minute, then uncover and stir. When the greens are a brilliant green, they are done. The rest is garnishing. Keep in mind a large bunch of any greens will shrink to next to nothing so plan accordingly and practice, until you understand how they cook.

My Hot Greens List Includes:

Beet greens, mustard greens, dandelion leaves, chickory, swiss chard, black kale, green kale, romaine lettuce, cabbage, bok choy greens and Asian greens. (For Asian greens go into china town and pick anything green. They are all great.) If you can't find organic greens you will probably be able to get them at the "Big Carrot" or "Whole Foods" stores in Toronto.

To the greens you can add a smidge of any of the following when you are cooking: tamari, sesame oil, olive oil, lemon juice.

Add toasted sesame seeds, black sesame seeds, or dulse when the greens are cooked, or just leave them bare.

Avocado Salad

Serves 4

"I call this avocado salad instead of quacamole because I like it chunky, not smooth. Purée it, add to it, leave something out, you really can't go wrong. Avocados are a gift from the gods, they don't need much assistance and are highly nutritious. They contain vitamins A, C, E and B6, potassium, folate, and dietary fiber. Wow!"

The key to this salad is to work fast. If you aren't serving immediately, cover tightly with plastic wrap and refrigerate or the avocados will discolour.

4	ripe organic avocados, peeled and pitted
4	plum tomatoes, seeded and cut in chunks
2 large	cloves garlic, minced
1-2 tsp	sea salt
½	lemon, juiced
	fresh ground pepper to taste

Optional: chopped cilantro, ¼ tsp of cumin or
chopped Italian parsley, ¼ tsp paprika

Put avocado flesh into a large bowl and immediately cover with the lemon juice. Using a sharp knife, cut the avocado into chunks. Add remaining ingredients and blend. Add more salt if desired. Salad should be more chunky than smooth. Serve immediately.

Brown Rice and Beet Salad

Serves 4-6

"This is one of the most requested recipes at Harmony Dawn. I think partially because it is visually stunning and secondly because it tastes absolutely amazing. I believe beets deserve an honored place at the table. They are high in antioxidants and vitamins, they detoxify our blood, and are our liver's best friend. They are also a beautiful rich, red colour."

3 cups	cooked brown rice	2 tsp	garlic, minced
2 tbsp	olive oil	1 tsp	sea salt
1	medium onion, chopped	¼ cup	pine nuts, toasted
4	medium red beets, peeled, cut into a ¼ inch dice reserving beet greens	1 tbsp	lemon zest or more
		½ cup	Italian parsley, chopped fresh pepper to taste
1 tsp	garlic salt	¼ cup	fresh lemon juice

In a large skillet heat oil over medium heat. Add onion and sauté for 5 minutes until tender. Add beets, garlic, salts, pepper and lemon juice, simmer, covered for about 25 minutes, stirring frequently. You may need to add water while cooking to prevent sticking. Beets are done when they can be easily pierced.

Remove from heat and toss in cooked brown rice, lemon zest, pine nuts and parsley, stirring to blend completely. Serve warm or at room temperature garnished with beet greens and sprinkled with lemon zest.

Mediterranean Chick Pea Salad

Serves 4

This salad is at its peak in the summer, although I can eat it year round. Served with organic greens, it is a satisfying lunch or casual dinner. Using canned beans makes preparation ultra easy, but dried beans are preferred. Use good quality olives such as Kalamata as they make a world of difference.

3	cups cooked chickpeas	2 tsp	dijon mustard
½ cup	sundried tomatoes, chopped	2 large	garlic cloves, minced
3	plum tomatoes, chopped	3 tbsp	balsamic vinegar
½ cup	fresh tarragon, chopped	½ cup	olive oil
½ cup	fresh basil, chopped		sea salt & fresh
¼ cup	fresh Italian parsley, chopped		ground pepper
12	black olives, pitted, chopped		

Drain and rinse chickpeas if using canned. If using dried, cover with water and let sit overnight. In the morning drain water and replace with fresh cold water to cover by 2 inches. Bring to a boil and simmer for 1½ hours until tender.

In a large bowl mix the chickpeas, tomatoes, herbs and olives.

In a small bowl whisk together the mustard, garlic, vinegar, salt and pepper. Add olive oil in a slow drizzle and whisk until emulsified. Dressing should be creamy.

Add dressing to the chick pea mixture and let sit for an hour stirring every 15 minutes. Taste and add more herbs if desired. Serve at room temperature.

Harmony Dawn Greek Salad

Serves 6

This is a bit of a twist on the traditional greek salad. The added green and yellow beans give a nice contrast to the tomatoes and peppers. This is always a favourite of mine because you can taste the sunshine in every bite, and at the same time, it is so cooling on a hot day.

Salad

2 cups	green and yellow beans, cut into 1 inch pieces
2	red peppers, seeded, cut into chunks
1	green pepper, seeded, cut into chunks
2 cups	grape tomatoes, halved
1	English cucumber, peeled, cut into chunks
1 large	red onion, sliced into slivers
1 cup	feta cheese, crumbled into thick chunks
¾ cup	Kalamata olives, pitted and halved
2 tbsp	capers

Dressing

2 cloves	garlic, minced
¼ cup	red wine vinegar
⅓ cup	extra virgin olive oil
2 tbsp	minced fresh basil
1 tsp	dried basil
1 tsp	dried oregano
	sea salt and fresh ground pepper

Bring a pot of water to a boil and cook beans for 5-7 minutes. Remove and place in a bowl of ice cold water for one minute. Drain and set aside.

In a large bowl place salad ingredients and toss together. In a small bowl whisk together the dressing ingredients until emulsified adding salt and pepper to taste.

Pour dressing over salad, toss and serve.

CHEF'S TIP:

Emulsification occurs when oil and vinegar are whisked together quickly, binding them together as one. The appearance should be creamy and not separated from one another.

Roasted Summer Corn Salad

Serves 4-6

In the middle of the summer we just can't get enough of corn, basil and tomatoes. The season is short but oh so sweet. Roasting the corn brings out its natural sweetness. This salad goes well paired with other summer fare like veggie burgers and big bountiful green salads.

6 cups	corn, preferably from fresh cobs
1 tbsp	olive oil
1	small red onion, sliced into circles
¼ cup	red wine vinegar
3 tbsp	honey
2 cups	sweet grape tomatoes, cut in half
2 tbsp	fresh lime juice
2 tbsp	chopped fresh marjoram or 2 tsp dried
2 tbsp	chopped fresh basil or 2 tsp dried
	sea salt & pepper

Preheat oven to 350°. Toss corn in olive oil, sprinkle with salt and pepper and roast on a baking sheet for 20 minutes until golden and fragrant.

In a small saucepan over medium heat, add vinegar and honey, bring to a boil and add onions, simmer for 3 minutes. Turn off heat and let sit for 15 minutes. Drain, reserving vinegar mixture.

Place corn in a large bowl, add lime juice, marjoram and basil, stir until combined. Add tomatoes, onion slices and 1 tbsp of wine vinegar mixture. Adjust seasonings and serve, garnished with edible flowers or marjoram leaves.

White Beans on Arugula

Serves 4

This salad tastes so fresh and spirited due to the lemon juice and fresh oregano. If you have time use dried beans instead of canned. You will need about 2 cups of cooked beans, or one 19 oz can.

2 cups	white kidney beans	2-3 tbsp	lemon juice + zest
3	green onions, thinly sliced	1-2 tsp	oregano, chopped
2	celery stalks, sliced	¼ tsp	sea salt & pepper
1 clove	garlic, minced	¼ cup	extra virgin olive oil
1 tsp	dijon mustard	1 bunch	fresh arugula, torn
1 tbsp	honey	¼ cup	parsley, chopped

Optional: 1 tin flaked light tuna, drained

If using canned beans, drain and rinse. Combine beans, onions and celery together in a large bowl.

In a small bowl, stir together garlic, mustard, honey, 2 tbsp of lemon juice, oregano, salt and pepper. Gradually whisk in oil. Pour over bean mixture and toss gently. Let stand at room temperature for half an hour to allow flavours to blend together.

If using tuna add it now. Taste and add remaining 1 tbsp of lemon juice if desired. Adjust salt to taste. Line a platter with the arugula. Top with the bean mixture and garnish with parsley and lemon zest.

Noodle Salad with Mango Lime Dressing

Serves 4-6

This is a Thai influenced salad, made with light vermicelli rice noodles, cooling mangoes and hot chilies. It is the perfect summer salad.

Salad

1 pkg	extra firm tofu cut into ½ inch cubes
2 tbsp	tamari
1 tbsp	sunflower oil
1 pkg	thin, rice vermicelli noodles
1	red pepper, sliced into slivers
1	bunch, green onions, sliced into slivers
3	carrots, julienned
1	bunch Thai basil, chopped

Dressing

1	mango, peeled, pitted & chopped
½ cup	sunflower oil
¼-½ tsp	dried chilies
2 tbsp	honey
½ tsp	sea salt & fresh ground pepper
	zest and juice of one lime

Preheat oven to 350°. In a bowl, mix together the tofu and tamari and marinate at least 4 hours. Oil the baking sheet and cook tofu until firm, approximately 15 to 20 minutes. Place noodles in a bowl, pour boiling water to cover and let sit for 10 minutes. Drain and set aside.

In a food processor, purée all dressing ingredients together until smooth.

In a large bowl, toss the noodles, peppers, onions, and carrots. Add tofu, dressing and basil and mix thoroughly. Garnish with lime wedges.

Funky Black Bean Salad with Corn

Serves 4-6

One of my favourite simple bean salad recipes. Serve at lunch with quesadillas, with a green salad or just on its own. It is tasty and crunchy, satisfying and highly nutritious. In a pinch, use canned beans but my preference is to always use dried beans.

1 tsp	dijon mustard		1	firm avocado
1 clove	garlic, minced		½ cup	red bell pepper, diced
2 tbsp	cider vinegar		1	carrot, diced - optional
2 tbsp	sunflower oil		2	green onions, thinly sliced
2 cups	cooked black beans			
2 cups	cooked corn		2 tbsp	fresh coriander, minced

In a small bowl whisk together the dressing ingredients, mustard, garlic, vinegar and oil until emulsified.

Peel, pit and dice the avocado, working quickly to avoid browning.

In a large bowl toss together all salad ingredients. Add dressing and combine thoroughly. Let sit for half an hour to blend flavours.

Thai Tofu Salad with Peanut Sauce

Serves 4-6

"I travelled to Thailand with my parents a couple of years ago and it was, without a doubt, the trip of a lifetime. I was seduced by the culture, the warmth and generosity of the people and the fabulous cuisine. I have been addicted to the aromas, spices, cooking techniques, and how simply they seem to prepare the most flavourful of dishes, ever since."

Salad

1 pkg	thin, rice vermicelli noodles
1 pkg	extra firm tofu, cut into ½ inch cubes
3 tbsp	tamari or Braggs
2 tbsp	sunflower oil
1	English cucumber, julienned
1½ cups	carrots, julienned

Dressing

4 cloves	garlic, minced	½ cup	peanut butter
1 tsp	salt	1¼ tsp	dried chilies
¼ cup	tamari or Braggs	¼ cup	sunflower oil
2 tbsp	lime juice	1 tbsp	maple syrup

Garnish: ¼ cup roasted, unsalted peanuts, coarsely chopped
¼ cup fresh coriander, chopped

Marinate the tofu, tamari and oil together in a bowl for at least 4 hours. Place on a baking sheet and bake in a 350° oven for 20 minutes until slightly crunchy.

Place noodles in a large bowl, pour boiling water to cover, let sit for 10 minutes. Drain and arrange on a platter.

In a large bowl combine the tofu, carrot and cucumbers.

Using a food processor to make the dressing, pulse the garlic and salt to form a paste.

Add remaining ingredients and purée until well combined. Mix half of the dressing with the tofu mixture and arrange on top of the noodles. Just before serving, pour remaining dressing over salad, followed by peanuts and coriander.

Sea Vegetable Salad

Serves 4-6

I try to use sea vegetables as much as possible, in salads, soups and stews. They are loaded with vitamins, minerals and flavour, so you don't need very much to satisfy. This salad combines sweet arame with the crunch of corn and snow peas in a savoury dressing. Serve on its own or with brown rice sushi (pg. 58) for a complete meal. Arame can be found in health food stores and Asian markets.

¾ cup	dried arame	1 cup	corn, cooked
2 tbsp	sunflower oil	½ cup	green onions, chopped
3 tbsp	lemon juice	½ cup	Italian parsley, chopped
1 large	clove garlic, minced	1 cup	snow peas
3 tbsp	Braggs	1 tbsp	sesame seeds, toasted
½ cup	each, diced carrots, red & green pepper		

Soak the arame in a large bowl covered with cold water. Let sit for 5 minutes, drain and set aside. Arame will lose its nutrients if left too long in water.

Remove the strings from the snow peas by cutting the ends off and pulling along the vein. This is the tough part of the pea that needs to be removed. Cut peas in ¼ inch pieces on the diagonal and blanch in boiling water for about 8 minutes. Remove and place in ice water (this helps retain colour and crunch). Drain and set aside.

In a small bowl, whisk together oil, lemon juice, garlic and Braggs. In a large bowl combine all salad ingredients. Add dressing and toss together. Let sit 30 minutes to let flavours combine. Garnish with sesame seeds.

Cannellini Bean Salad

Serves 4-6

This is a tasty, hearty salad, with an extra flavour boost from the egg. Serve with salad greens on a platter, with a warm baguette. Cannellini beans are a small white bean with a subtle flavour (substitute navy beans if unavailable). For this salad I always boil the beans as I rarely find them in canned form.

2 cups	cannellini beans, cooked
1	tomato, diced
1	egg, hard boiled & coarsely chopped
2 tbsp	red onion, chopped
2 tbsp	Italian parsley chopped
2 tbsp	sundried tomatoes, chopped
2 tbsp	olive oil
1 tbsp	white wine vinegar
1-2	cloves garlic, minced
4-5	Kalamata olives, coarsely chopped
2	spring onions, chopped fine
	sea salt and pepper

In a medium bowl, combine beans, tomato, egg, onion, parsley and sundried tomatoes.

In a small bowl whisk the olive oil, vinegar and garlic until emulsified. Pour over the bean mixture to coat. Stir in the olives, salt and pepper.

Cover and let stand for an hour to blend flavours or refrigerate 4-5 hours and bring to room temperature. Sprinkle with the spring onions and serve.

Quinoa and Vegetable Salad

Serves 6

Quinoa is an exquisite, ancient grain. When cooked, it has a beautiful little ring around it and a lovely nutty flavour. It is high in protein and alkaline, which makes it easier to digest for people with sensitivities. A lot of packaged foods we eat in North America are overly salty and contain high amounts of sugar. Both are acidic and create heat in our bodies. Disease and cancer thrive in an acidic environment, so eating foods that are alkaline helps to create balance in our bodies.

Salad

2 cups	Quinoa		½ cup	zucchini, diced
1 tsp	sea salt		1 cup	cooked chick peas
3 cups	water		¾ cup	sultanas
1½ cups	carrots, diced		¾ cup	almond slivers, toasted
½ cup	red onion, diced		½ cup	green onions, chopped
1½ cups	red & yellow peppers, diced			

Dressing

¾ cup	olive oil		1 tsp	sea salt
½ cup	lemon juice		½ tsp	white pepper
½ cup	Italian parsley, chopped		¾ tsp	cinnamon
¼ cup	fresh mint, chopped		¼ tsp	nutmeg

Wash quinoa well in several changes of water. Bring salted water to a boil, add quinoa. Cover, reduce heat to a simmer for approximately 10 to 15 minutes. Remove from heat, drain any excess water.

In a small bowl, whisk together the dressing ingredients.

In a large bowl combine all vegetables and quinoa while still warm. Add dressing and mix well. Garnish with green onions.

Curried Tofu Salad with Mango & Cashews

Serves 6

"I love mangoes. Every time I serve them in salads or dressings, they give me a feeling of summer, any month of the year, like a ray of sunshine is alive in my mouth. You can easily substitute tempeh for the tofu if you prefer."

2 pkgs	extra firm tofu, cut into ½ inch cubes	4	green onions, minced
3 tbsp	tamari	¼ cup	plain yoghurt
2 tbsp	sunflower oil	¼ cup	mayonnaise
2 tbsp	lemon juice	1½ tsp	curry powder
1 cup	celery, chopped	½ tsp	ground cumin
2	mangoes, peeled, pitted, & cut into ½ inch cubes	1 cup	unsalted cashews, roasted
		2 tbsp	fresh coriander, chopped

Combine the tofu, tamari and oil, marinate for a minimum of 4 hours. Place on a baking sheet and bake in a 350° oven for 20 minutes.

In a large bowl, toss together the tofu, mango, lemon juice, celery and scallions.

In a small bowl whisk together the yoghurt, mayonnaise, curry powder and cumin. Add to tofu bowl and combine thoroughly. Add salt and pepper to taste.

Coarsely chop cashews and just before serving add nuts and coriander to salad. Serve at room temperature or chilled.

Steamed Vegetables with Dulse

Serves 6

Simple, colourful and nutritious is how to describe this salad. Dulse flakes are a highly nutritious sea vegetable and can be sprinkled on salads, used in soups or dressings and as a garnish. Serve with tahini sesame dressing (pg.102) for an alkaline macrobiotic dish.

1 bunch	broccoli cut into small florets, stems peeled and cut into chunks
1 head	cauliflower cut into small florets
2	sweet potatoes, cut into ½ inch circles
6 large	swiss chard leaves, shredded
1 tbsp	tamari or Braggs
2 tsp	dulse flakes
1 tsp	sesame seeds, toasted

Steam the sweet potatoes for 25 minutes until firm tender.

Meanwhile using a wok or a deep skillet, bring ½ cup water with tamari to a boil and cook the broccoli and cauliflower until broccoli is bright green and tender. Add swiss chard and cook another 30 seconds.

Remove from heat and spoon vegetables out. Place in a large bowl and surround top of bowl with sweet potato circles. Sprinkle with dulse and sesame seeds. Serve hot.

CHEF'S TIP:

Sweet potatoes react to metal and turn black in parts. Using a non-metallic steamer will eliminate this.

To shred swiss chard, roll leaves tightly together and cut through layers.

Roasted Summer Vegetable Platter

Serves 4-6

" I love roasting vegetables and most people I have met love them also. The natural sweetness of the vegetables is just irresistible. Any combination of summer vegetables works well, so play around with what you have available to you and see the magic unfold. "

2 heads	garlic, cut in half horizontally
4	golden beets, quartered
1 lb	young green beans
1 lb	asparagus spears, stalks trimmed
1	fennel bulb, fronds removed, quartered
2	radicchio bulbs, quartered
1	Vidalia onion, cut into sections
¼ cup	olive oil
2 tbsp	maple syrup
2 tbsp	balsamic vinegar
1 tsp	sea salt and freshly ground pepper

Preheat oven to 425°. Place the garlic and beets in a piece of foil, sprinkle with salt, pepper and a drizzle of olive oil. Seal and roast for 40 minutes until soft. Remove from oven and let sit until remaining vegetables are cooked. When cooled slightly, remove skins from beets by rubbing gently.

Turn oven down to 350°. In a small bowl whisk together oil, maple syrup and balsamic vinegar. Cover baking sheets with foil to prevent sticking and place vegetables on the sheet. Coat with the sauce and sprinkle with salt and pepper. Cook, turning vegetables once, approximately 20-30 minutes until tender. Arrange all vegetables on a large platter and serve hot or at room temperature.

Autumn Roasted Root Vegetable Platter

Serves 6

"This is a beautiful, colourful display of nature's autumn bounty. It is a real crowd pleaser and it is equally good served hot or at room temperature. Roasting vegetables brings out their natural sweetness. Serve with fig dressing for a match made in heaven. Use any combination of vegetables, but keep the sizes similar or cooking times will vary."

3	red beets quartered, reserving beet greens
2 heads	garlic, cut in half horizontally
10	small carrots
10	small parsnips
1 small	acorn squash cut in half, seeds removed, cut into ½ inch slices
½ small	butternut squash cut in half, seeds removed, cut into ½ inch slices
½ small	cauliflower, cut into small florets
1 large	red onion cut into quarters
	olive oil, sea salt, fresh ground pepper
	fresh rosemary sprigs

Preheat oven to 425°. Place beets in foil, sprinkle with salt and pepper and a teaspoon of olive oil. Place garlic in a separate piece of foil with open cloves side up, sprinkle with salt and pepper and olive oil.

Place both packages on a cookie sheet and bake for 40 minutes. Remove from oven when fragrant and tender. Leave in foil while you prepare the rest of the vegetables.

Reduce heat to 350°. Lightly brush olive oil on a large baking sheet. You may need 2 sheets. Place all vegetables neatly on the sheets. Brush with olive oil, sprinkle with salt and pepper and place in oven. After about 20 minutes or when vegetables look light brown turn them over and bake the other side.

Open beet package and lightly rub to remove skins.

Assembling

On a large platter begin assembling the vegetables. Start by laying the beet greens, followed by the vegetables, grouping each vegetable together so the platter looks abundant and colourful.

Garnish with rosemary sprigs and serve on their own or with fig dressing (pg.103).

Vegetable Antipasti Platter

Serves 4

Antipasti means appetizers. These dishes are great accompaniments to summer veggie burgers, as part of a tapas platter, or served as individual side dishes with organic greens and warm baguette. Place vegetables on a large serving platter, garnished with parsley.

Warm Chickpeas with Herbs and Garlic

3 tbsp	olive oil
2 cups	cooked chickpeas, or one 19 oz can
3 tbsp	minced garlic
1 tsp	each, dried basil, oregano, marjoram
¼ cup	chopped fresh Italian parsley
½ tsp	sea salt
	freshly ground pepper

Heat oil in a large skillet over medium high heat. Add garlic and cook until sizzling and golden brown. Add chickpeas, dried herbs, salt and lots of ground pepper. Cook until chickpeas are heated through, adding more olive oil to prevent sticking. Add parsley, toss and place on serving dish.

Grilled Summer Zucchini

For this you will need a grill frying pan, or use the BBQ.

2 -3	six inch green zucchini
	cut into 2 inch long, ½ inch thick pieces
	olive oil, sea salt and fresh ground pepper

Over medium high heat, brush pan with olive oil and place the zucchini in pan. Sprinkle with salt and pepper. Cook until you see lovely grill marks and then flip and cook the other side. Zucchini is a wet vegetable so try not to over cook them or they will be mushy. Place on serving dish.

Grape Tomatoes with Basil and Garlic

Serves 4

This is a great with a warm baguette, added to a green salad, or served as part of an antipasti platter. Add chickpeas to the sauté and create a hearty, warm summer salad.

1 pkg	red grape tomatoes, left whole
2 tbsp	olive oil
1½ tbsp	minced garlic
¼ cup	fresh basil, chopped
	sea salt & fresh ground pepper

In a skillet over high heat, add the oil and cook garlic until golden brown. Add tomatoes and shake pan to roll the tomatoes in the garlic and cook until almost bursting. You will see the skins expand. Add salt, pepper and basil and serve garnished with a big basil leaf or basil flower.

Garlic Rosemary Potatoes

Serves 4-6

Roasted potatoes are pure heaven in my book. They go with just about anything from sandwiches to veggie burgers, it really doesn't matter. One thing to keep in mind when purchasing potatoes and other root vegetables, is to buy organic if possible. All vegetables are sprayed with enormous amounts of pesticides and herbicides, all of which are toxic to humans and animals.

6 large	Yukon gold potatoes, cut into ½ inch cubes
2 tbsp	olive oil
1 tsp	fresh lemon juice
½ tsp	sea salt
½ tsp	freshly ground pepper
2 tbsp	finely chopped fresh rosemary, plus sprigs for garnish
2 tbsp	finely chopped garlic

Preheat oven to 350°.

Scrub and peel the potatoes if they aren't organic.

In a large bowl combine all ingredients. Toss gently to cover potatoes with the herbs and place on a large baking sheet. Bake for 45 minutes, turning the potatoes once after 25 minutes (they tend to stick if you turn more frequently).

Potatoes are done when they are a nice golden brown and crunchy. Garnish with extra rosemary sprigs.

Sesame Sweet Potato Wedges

Serves 4-6

Serve with wraps, sandwiches, chili, or as a late night snack with peanut dressing (pg.95).

4	sweet potatoes, cut lengthwise into thick wedges
2 tbsp	olive oil
2 tbsp	toasted sesame oil
1 tbsp	sesame seeds, toasted
1 tbsp	toasted peanuts, chopped fine
	sea salt
	cilantro leaves for garnish

Preheat oven to 400°.

In a large bowl, toss the potatoes, oils and sesame seeds. Spread on a baking sheet and sprinkle with a touch of salt. Roast for 30 minutes until crisp tender. Sprinkle with chopped peanuts and cilantro leaves.

CHEF'S TIP:

Toxins from pesticides soak into the skins of vegetables and can leech into our systems if not removed. Unfortunately this is where a lot of nutrients reside.

"Creamy" Strawberry Vinaigrette

Makes about 2 cups

This dressing is always a hit with the ladies. Pink, pretty and wonderfully fragrant, it goes well with salad greens or over ice cream. That's right ice cream. Keeps well for 2 weeks, refrigerated. In season Ontario strawberries are soft, luscious, sweet, fragrant and everything a strawberry is supposed to be, which is quite unlike what you find in the grocery store out of season.

2 cups	fresh Ontario strawberries
3 tbsp	raspberry balsamic vinegar
3 tbsp	maple syrup
¼ tsp	sea salt
¼ tsp	white pepper
¾ cup	sunflower oil

Lightly wash and dry strawberries, remove core.

In a food processor, purée strawberries until smooth and creamy. Add remaining ingredients except oil and blend thoroughly.

Add oil in a slow steady stream until dressing is smooth and creamy. Taste and adjust seasonings. If dressing is too thick, add a tablespoon or so of water until desired consistency.

CHEF'S TIP:

Vinegars such as raspberry, fig, champagne, grapeseed, walnut and balsamic, can be found in most supermarkets or specialty shops.

Peanut Salad Dressing

Makes about 1 cup

This dressing is beautiful served over simple salad greens, warm Asian greens or steamed vegetables. Cut back on the water to make a lovely thick dipping sauce.

1½ tbsp	toasted sesame oil	6 tbsp	water
3 cloves	garlic, minced	2 tbsp	tamari
1 tbsp	grated ginger, optional	1½ tbsp	maple syrup
¼ tsp	ground cumin	pinch	cayenne, salt, tobasco
¼ tsp	ground coriander	¼ cup	toasted peanuts,
½ cup	organic peanut butter		coarsely ground

In a small saucepan, heat sesame oil over medium high heat. Add garlic, ginger, cumin and coriander and cook until lightly browned, approximately 4 minutes.

In a small bowl, combine the peanut butter and water, tamari and maple syrup. Add more water if too thick, consistency should be smooth and able to pour with a ladle.

Add the sesame oil mixture and blend thoroughly. One at a time add cayenne, salt and tobasco, tasting after each until desired flavour and heat are achieved.

Add the ground peanuts for a thicker consistency if desired.

Roasted Shallot Dressing

Makes about 1 cup

This dressing can be served over salad greens, roasted vegetables or steamed greens. It is a terrific all season dressing that just improves with age.

4 large	shallots		2 tbsp	water
3 garlic	cloves		¾ cup	olive oil
2 tbsp	balsamic vinegar		½ tsp	sea salt
1 tsp	dijon mustard		½ tsp	freshly ground pepper
2 tbsp	maple syrup			

Preheat oven to 375°.

Peel shallots and garlic cloves and place in a piece of foil. Sprinkle with olive oil and a dash of salt and pepper. Seal loosely and bake approximately 45 minutes.

In a food processor, add shallots, garlic, balsamic vinegar, mustard, maple syrup and water. Purée until smooth and creamy. Add olive oil in a slow, steady stream blending for about a minute. Add salt and pepper to taste.

Adjust seasonings, adding more maple syrup and dijon mustard to taste. If dressing is too thick, add a little bit more water.

Peach Tarragon Vinaigrette

Makes about 1½ cups

I love using nature's bounty in the summer. The abundance of fruit and vegetables from our local farmers is pure heaven. This dressing is a beautiful, golden colour and works well served over salad greens, alongside spicy entrées.

3 large	Ontario peaches, peeled and pitted
3 cloves	garlic, minced
1 tbsp	fresh tarragon, minced
½ cup	sunflower oil
2-3 tbsp	lime juice
1½ tbsp	each lemon juice, honey and dijon mustard
⅛ tsp	white pepper
	sea salt to taste

The best way to remove the skins of peaches is to blanch them. Make an X in the base of the peach with a sharp knife and drop into boiling water for 3 minutes. Remove and immerse immediately into a cold water bath. Skins will just rub off.

In a blender or food processor, purée peaches until completely smooth. Add remaining ingredients and blend thoroughly. Taste, and adjust seasonings to taste.

Poppy Honey Dressing

Makes about 2 cups

This dressing works well with bitter greens, spicy mustard greens, spinach, steamed kale and steamed swiss chard.

1	large shallot, minced	½ cup	cider vinegar
1 small	garlic clove, minced	¾ cup	sunflower oil
1 tbsp	mayo or nayo	2 tbsp	poppy seeds
½ cup	honey		sea salt & fresh pepper to taste

In a food processor, combine all the ingredients except the oil and poppy seeds and blend until smooth. Add the oil in a slow stream while the motor is running, blending until smooth and emulsified. Add the poppy seeds and pulse until combined.

Creamy Sundried Tomato Dressing

Makes about 1½ cups

½ cup	sundried tomatoes, chopped	2 tbsp	tamari
¼ tsp	tobasco sauce	4 tbsp	cider vinegar
2 tsp	dijon mustard	1 tbsp	honey
1 tsp	dried basil	½ cup	olive oil
1 tsp	minced garlic	½ cup	sunflower oil
½ tsp	capers, minced		sea salt & fresh pepper

Purée all ingredients in food processor or blender until emulsified and creamy. If too thick, add up to ¼ cup of water. Taste and adjust seasonings.

Orange Raspberry Dressing

Makes about 2 cups

This dressing works well paired with spicy dishes like Moroccan Vegetable Tagine (pg.177). Raspberry vinegar can be found in specialty stores and some supermarkets.

2	shallots, minced
zest	of one organic orange
2	freshly squeezed oranges or 1½ cups of juice
4 tbsp	raspberry vinegar
⅓ cup	tahini
1 tsp	orange concentrate
1 tsp	sea salt
¾ cup	sunflower oil

In a shallow saucepan bring the orange juice to a boil. Reduce heat and simmer until reduced to half. Remove from heat and allow to cool.

In a food processor or blender, purée shallots, zest, raspberry vinegar, orange concentrate, salt and tahini until smooth. Add the orange juice reduction.

In a stream, add the sunflower oil and blend until creamy and slightly thickened. If necessary adjust the amount of tahini, which will make it creamier.

Taste the dressing. Adjust the seasonings.

Roasted Garlic Fig Dressing

Makes about 1¾ cups

This is a versatile dressing that is rich and creamy. It can be paired with fish or vegetables. Roasting vegetables brings out their natural sweetness and flavour. Fig balsamic vinegar can be found in specialty stores and some supermarkets.

3 heads	garlic
2	black mission figs, chopped
2 tbsp	water
1 tsp	dijon mustard
2 tbsp	maple syrup, or to taste
¼ cup	fig balsamic vinegar
1½ cups	sunflower oil
	sea salt & fresh pepper to taste

Preheat oven to 350°. Cut tops of the garlic heads to expose the bulbs and sprinkle with olive oil, salt and pepper, and place on a piece of foil. Wrap loosely and bake about 45 minutes until fragrant and soft and the garlic has darkened in colour.

Using a food processor or blender, purée the garlic, figs and water until creamy. Add dijon, maple syrup and vinegar and pulse until combined. With motor running, add the sunflower oil in an even stream until the dressing is nice and creamy. Add salt and pepper, taste and adjust seasonings.

Shiitake Sesame Dressing

Makes about 1¾ cups

This is a Harmony Dawn favourite. Flavourful and savoury, with a hint of sweetness, it can be paired with salads and warm vegetables. Chinese 5-spice seasoning can be found in most supermarkets.

5	dried shiitake mushrooms	1 tbsp	sesame oil
1 clove	garlic, minced	1 tsp	tamari
½ tsp	Chinese 5-spice seasoning	½ tsp	sea salt
⅛ cup	maple syrup	1 cup	sunflower oil, approx.
¼ cup	rice wine vinegar		

In a saucepan, cover shiitakes with water and bring to a boil. Reduce heat to a simmer and cook for 15 minutes, until soft. Cover and let sit another 15 minutes. Remove shiitakes, press out excess liquid, reserving cooking water. Chop shiitakes, removing hard stems.

In a food processor, blend chopped shiitakes and garlic until minced. Add all ingredients except sunflower oil and the cooking water. Blend until well combined.

With motor running, add sunflower oil in a stream until emulsified, dressing may be thick so add shiitake water a tablespoon at a time until dressing is of desired consistency.

Tahini Sesame Dressing

Makes about 1½ cups

⅔ cup	soy milk
2 tsp	garlic, minced
1 tbsp	tamari or Braggs
1 tbsp	sesame oil
½ cup	tahini
½ tsp	sea salt, or to taste

Combine all ingredients in a blender or food processor and blend until smooth and creamy. The dressing will thicken while it sits due to the tahini.

Variation

Omit sesame oil and soy milk. Add ¼ cup lemon juice, 2 tbsp water and 1 tsp of lemon zest for a zippy, fresh dressing.

Roasted Beet and Fig Dressing

Makes about 1½ cups

"This is a fun, intensely flavoured dressing that is full of colour. I had an abundance of beets and wondered what to do with them. I fell asleep and this came to me. It is now one of Harmony Dawn's favourites. Using whole vegetables as dressings is a great way to increase the nutritional quotient."

2	beets, roasted	3 tbsp	fig balsamic vinegar
5	black mission figs	½ tsp	sea salt
3	cloves garlic, minced	½ tsp	white pepper
1 tsp	dijon mustard	¾ cup	olive oil
2 tbsp	maple syrup		water

Preheat oven to 350°.

Quarter beets and place on a piece of foil. Sprinkle with salt, pepper and a touch of olive oil. Secure foil and roast in oven for approximately 45 minutes, until beets are tender.

In a food processor, purée beets. Add remaining ingredients except oil and water and blend until minced and combined. Add oil and blend 2 or 3 minutes until smooth, adding water a tablespoon at a time if too thick. Dressing should be creamy and a lovely shade of maroon. Adjust seasonings.

"Creamy" Tarragon Vinaigrette

Makes about 2 cups

Tarragon is one of my all time favourite herbs and it's so versatile! Thankfully, it is abundant in our gardens and I use it in dressings, sauces, salads, sprinkled on white fleshed fish (in fact, just about anything). My good friend and fellow garden lover, Gabi, makes a wonderful tarragon vinegar, which is what I used in this recipe. However, you can buy commercially prepared tarragon vinegar in most supermarkets.

1 large	shallot, minced
1 large	garlic clove, minced
1 cup	packed fresh tarragon
2 tsp	dijon mustard
2 tbsp	honey
¼ cup	tarragon vinegar
1 tsp	sea salt
1½ cups	sunflower oil

Put all ingredients except oil into food processor and blend until well combined. Add oil in a steady stream and blend until emulsified. The dressing will become a lovely shade of green.

Roasted Golden Onion Dressing

Makes about 1½ cups

> "This dressing is a wonderful concoction from one of my cooking workshops. It was autumn and I had pre-roasted the onions because I felt they would make a great base. With a little direction on dressing basics, the lovely ladies, Jen, Frances, Cara, Mom and Christine, did the rest. It is fabulous!"

3	medium yellow onions, quartered
1 tsp	dijon mustard
1 tbsp	maple syrup
3 tbsp	balsamic vinegar
½ tsp	sea salt
1 cup	olive oil

Optional: ¼ tsp dried sage or dried thyme

Preheat oven to 350°.

Place onions in a piece of foil, sprinkle with salt and pepper and a touch of olive oil. Wrap loosely, and roast on a baking sheet for 45 minutes or until fragrant and caramelized.

Place onions in food processor and blend until puréed. Add mustard, maple syrup, vinegar and salt. In a stream, add olive oil and purée until rich and creamy. Taste and add sage or thyme, if desired.

4

SAUCES DIPS & FUN STUFF

Basics of Marinades

Marinades are an easy way to enhance the flavour of tofu, tempeh and fish. Ideally they should be quick to prepare and require only a few ingredients.

The combinations for marinades are limited only by your imagination. A basic approach is to mix and match sweet, savoury, salty, spicy, and sour flavours, keeping in mind the colours and textures of the final product. Here are a few simple elements to help you put together your unique marinades.

Sour Flavours Include:

Vinegars such as balsamic, cider, white wine, red wine and champagne, wines such as chardonnay, madeira, merlot, pinot noir, mirin, port and sherry.

Acidic Juices Include:

Apple, lemon, lime, orange, peach, pineapple, roasted pepper purée, all fruit zests.

Savoury Thickening Agents Include:

Miso – all varieties, mustard, mashed chickpeas, peanut butter, tahini, nut butters, pesto, tomato paste, marmite.

Sweetening Agents Include:

Honey, maple syrup, molasses, rice syrup, barley syrup, sucanet.

Herbs and Spices Include:

Chives, cilantro, garlic, ginger, lemon grass, chilies, scallions, shallots, basil, bay leaf, dill, fennel, marjoram, oregano, rosemary, sage, sorrel, tarragon, thyme, caraway, celery seed, chili powder, cinnamon, coriander, cumin, mustard, curry powder, onion powder, anise, nutmeg.

Oils and Condiments Include:

Olive oil, sesame oil, sunflower oil, peanut oil, horseradish, hot sauces, nutritional yeast, sea salt, pepper, tamari, Braggs, wasabi, worcestershire sauce, hoisin sauce, sambal oelek, curry paste, chili paste.

BBQ Marinating Sauce

Makes 2½ cups

There are a lot of ingredients in this sauce but it is very tasty and quite versatile. It can be used for tempeh, tofu or even shrimp and as a basting sauce while cooking, for heartier flavour. Keeps well, refrigerated for a week.

¼ cup	white vinegar		1 cup	organic ketchup
½ cup	water		¾ cup	white onion, minced
1 tbsp	unsalted butter		1 large	garlic clove, minced
2 tbsp	honey		1 tbsp	fresh lemon juice
1 tsp	dry hot mustard		½ tsp	freshly ground pepper
1	bay leaf		1 tsp	sea salt
3 tbsp	worcestershire sauce		½ tsp	cayenne
½ cup	tomato purée		¼ tsp	dried chilies

In a saucepan over medium heat, combine all ingredients, bring to a boil stirring constantly and simmer for 15 minutes.

Pour over tempeh or tofu and let marinate several hours.

CHEF'S TIP:

Vegetarian worcestershire sauce can be purchased at health or natural food stores. For a more intense flavour, substitute molasses for the sweetener but decrease to 1 tbsp.

Simple and Basic Marinade

Makes ½ cup

Simple, multiple use marinade, for tofu, tempeh, fish.

¼ cup	tamari
2	cloves garlic, minced
1 inch	piece ginger, peeled and finely grated
2 tsp	maple syrup
¼ cup	water
1 tbsp	miso

Combine all ingredients in a blender or food processor. Pour over items to be marinated and let sit for a minimum of 1 hour to overnight in the refrigerator.

Lemon Pepper Marinade

Makes 1 cup

I use this marinade primarily with tempeh which can handle the tartness of the lemon.

2 tsp	dried chilies
2 tsp	dried oregano
½ cup	fresh lemon juice
1 tbsp	freshly ground pepper
⅓ cup	olive oil

Blend all ingredients in a blender until well combined.

Mint Yoghurt Marinade

Makes 1½ cups

This is perfect for tofu, fish or shrimp and curry inspired menus. Pour over items and marinate overnight in the refrigerator.

¼ cup	fresh mint leaves, minced
1 tsp	honey
1 tsp	garlic, minced
2 tsp	lemon juice
2 tbsp	sunflower oil
1 cup	plain yoghurt

Blend all ingredients in a blender until well combined.

Teriyaki Marinade

Makes 1 cup

Use for tofu, tempeh, shrimp and vegetables. Mirin is Japanese sweet rice wine and can be found in Asian stores, health food stores and specialty stores.

⅔ cup	tamari
¼ cup	mirin
5 tbsp	cider vinegar
½ cup	maple syrup
2 tbsp	fresh ginger root, chopped

In a saucepan combine all the ingredients, bring to a boil and simmer until it is reduced to 1 cup, stirring frequently. Strain through a sieve into a bowl and let cool. Proceed with recipe.

Hoisin Sauce

Makes 1 cup

I like to use this sauce for marinating and roasting green beans, cauliflower, carrots, fennel (pretty much anything really). Green beans take longer than most vegetables and depending on the age of the bean, they can be chewy. Use young fresh beans and taste at the 20 minute mark.

⅓ cup	hoisin sauce	½ tsp	dried chilies
⅓ cup	orange juice, or one orange	1 tbsp	chives, chopped
2 tbsp	tamari	1 tbsp	sesame seeds,
2 tbsp	olive oil		toasted
	fresh ground pepper to taste		

In a small bowl, stir together all the ingredients except herbs and sesame seeds.

Add vegetables that you are marinating and let sit for 15 minutes.

Preheat oven to 400°. Place vegetables on a large baking sheet and roast for 20 to 30 minutes depending on vegetable, checking every 10 minutes.

Arrange on a platter. Sprinkle with chives and sesame seeds and serve hot or at room temperature.

Hot Chili Basting Sauce

Makes about 1½ cup

This is really hot due to the jalapeno pepper. The ginger, coriander and lime add a freshness to the heat. Use to baste tofu, shrimp and fish. Feel free to add more jalapenos if you want but wear gloves when handling as the seeds are what contain the stinging heat.

1 large	jalapeno pepper, minced, including some of the seeds
½ cup	shallots, minced
1 large	garlic clove, minced
¼ cup	chopped fresh coriander leaves and stems
1 tbsp	ginger root, peeled and minced
½ tsp	turmeric
¾ cup	tomato purée
2 tbsp	lime juice

Purée all ingredients in a food processor and add a touch of salt to taste.

Lightly baste at the beginning, midway and towards the end of cooking (that way the sauce gets cooked into dish).

Simple Tomato Sauce

Makes about 3 cups

The beauty of this sauce is in its simplicity; fresh Ontario summer tomatoes in their prime, captured in a sauce. Add fresh herbs like basil, oregano, tarragon or leave it plain.

If you prefer to have a chunky sauce, remove skins by cutting an x in the base and blanching in hot water. After placing in an ice bath, skins will slip off. Proceed with the recipe but do not run through the food mill.

4   lbs very ripe Ontario tomatoes, stemmed and quartered

In a heavy pot, combine the tomatoes with ½ cup of water, or enough to just cover the bottom of the kettle and bring the mixture to a boil over moderate heat. Simmer, partly covered for 5 to 20 minutes or until the tomatoes have softened and begin to fall apart.

Transfer the tomato mixture to a large fine sieve set over a bowl and let it drain until it is cooled to room temperature. Discard the liquid in the bowl and force the tomatoes through a food mill or a large sieve.

Sauce can be frozen until needed or canned using proper canning techniques.

Roasted Red Pepper Cream Sauce

Makes about 2 cups

This sauce is great with burgers, stuffed into pitas or used as a dip for vegetables (hot and cold). You can omit the tofu for a less creamy version.

3 large	red peppers, roasted
1 head	of garlic, roasted
2	garlic cloves, minced
1 pkg	silken tofu, blue tetrapack
½ cup	extra virgin olive oil
1 tsp	salt
½ tsp	white pepper

Optional: ½ tsp dried chilies

Preheat oven to 425°.

Slice top off garlic and place in a piece of foil, sprinkle with salt, pepper and a touch of olive oil. Put on a large, lightly oiled baking sheet along with the peppers. Roast the garlic for about 40 minutes until soft. Let cool and remove garlic cloves.

The peppers will roast more quickly but you will have to turn them every so often. Remove the peppers when all sides are black. Place in a covered bowl to steam and cool. Peel skins off and remove seeds.

Purée all ingredients in a food processor until smooth and creamy. Adjust salt and pepper and add chilies if using.

Fig Balsamic Sauce

Makes about 1 cup

This sauce is pure decadence. Black mission figs are a little bit sweet, with a rich, wonderfully textured flavour. Pair this with roasted autumn root vegetables (pg.88) for a match made in heaven.

7 large	black mission figs, chopped fine
¼ cup	fig balsamic vinegar
2 tbsp	maple syrup
¼ cup	olive oil
	sea salt & water

Using a food processor, blend figs with about 2 tablespoons of water until smooth (it will be thick).

Add remaining ingredients and blend until smooth and creamy. If you want to make a thinner dressing, add a bit more water. Taste and adjust seasoning.

CHEF'S TIP:

When making sauces, leave them in the food processor for a couple of hours to allow flavours to develop before adjusting seasonings. Garlic becomes a lot stronger as it sits, so a little goes a long way.

Shiitake Tahini Sauce

Makes about 1 cup

This sauce is perfect with tofu steaks or steamed vegetables. It will keep for 2 weeks, refrigerated. Bring to room temperature to serve. The sauce will thicken as it sits, so add a touch of water and blend in food processor.

⅔ cup	tahini
1 tbsp	sesame oil
¼ cup	tamari
1 cup	dry shiitake mushrooms
3	garlic cloves
	sea salt to taste

Place shiitakes in a saucepan with water to cover. Bring to a boil and simmer for 20 minutes until soft. Drain, reserving cooking water. Chop the mushrooms into small fine pieces, removing stems.

In a blender or food processor, blend all ingredients until smooth and creamy. If sauce is too thick add a smidge of the reserved cooking water.

Spicy Beet Sauce

Makes about 1 cup

> This is one of my all time favourites. When I use red beets the sauce becomes a sensuous, pinky, red colour and if I use golden beets, it is a bright, sunny, gold colour. Full of flavour, it can be used with crudités, as a sauce for burgers, in pitas or wraps and as a base for bruschetta. It is pure health food full of "liver loving" nutrients. You won't be able to stop eating it.

Golden beets can be found in organic markets. They are slightly sweeter than red beets. If you mix them with red beets they will take on the red colour. For a more intense flavour, roast the garlic and beets, wrapped in foil and baked in a 425° oven for 45 minutes, then proceed with recipe.

3	red or golden beets about 1½ cups, peeled and cut into ½ inch cubes
1 cup	cooked chick peas
¼ cup	hazelnuts, toasted
4	cloves of garlic
½ cup	olive oil
2 tbsp	lemon juice
	dried chilies to taste
	sea salt & fresh pepper to taste

Place beets in a small saucepan and just cover with water. Bring to a boil and simmer until tender. Drain.

In a food processor combine beets, chickpeas, hazelnuts and garlic. Purée until smooth. With motor running, add olive oil and lemon juice. Add salt, pepper and chilies, adjusting seasonings to taste. If you want a thinner sauce add more olive oil.

Salsa Romesco

Makes about 3 cups

This is a versatile summer sauce. There are many versions of salsa romesco, all using a variation of nuts, herbs and tomatoes. Think of it as pesto without the basil. It's fabulous with tofu steaks, vegetable burgers, fish, as a dip with crudités, on pitas, with steamed potatoes – the list goes on.

½ cup	pine nuts	2 tsp	paprika
½ cup	hazelnuts	½ tsp	sea salt
4	garlic cloves	½ cup	olive oil
1 tsp	dried chilies	3 tbsp	wine vinegar
4	plum tomatoes, seeded, pulp removed and quartered	4 tbsp	Italian parsley, chopped

In a preheated 350° oven, toast the pine nuts and hazelnuts for about 10 minutes, until fragrant. Let the nuts cool slightly, then using a tea towel, rub off the skins from the hazelnuts as best you can.

In a food processor, blend nuts, garlic and chilies until mixed. Add tomatoes, salt and paprika and blend until combined. Add olive oil and vinegar and blend to a smooth texture. Add parsley.

Let sit for 15 minutes and then adjust seasonings.

Caponata

Makes about 3 cups

This is a yummy, full flavoured dip. I have served it often at dinner parties and it packs a savoury punch with homemade crackers, crudités or bread sticks. Cocoa is an interesting touch, making the caponata richer in colour and consistency and also enhancing the flavours.

2 large	eggplants about 2½ lbs	1½ cups	tomato sauce
½ cup	olive oil	½ cup	white wine vinegar
1	onion, sliced thin	2 tbsp	sucanet
6 ribs	celery, cut into ½ inch pieces	½ cup	slivered almonds,
1 cup	green olives, pitted, chopped		toasted
½ cup	bottled capers, drained	2 tbsp	dutch process cocoa
	sea salt & fresh pepper		

Cut the eggplants into ¾ inch cubes. In a colander, toss them with a generous amount of sea salt and let drain for 1 hour. This will get rid of the bitterness that comes with the eggplants. Rinse the eggplant well and pat dry on paper towels. Blanch celery in boiling water for 1 minute, immerse in cold water and set aside.

In a large deep skillet, heat olive oil over high heat and fry the eggplant in small batches, stirring for 2 to 3 minutes or until golden and tender. Transfer and drain on paper towels.

In the same skillet, cook onion over medium heat until it is golden. Add celery and cook for about a minute. Stir in olives, capers, tomato sauce, vinegar, sucanet and cocoa powder. Simmer, stirring occasionally for about 5 minutes. Add the eggplants and simmer for an additional 10 minutes. Season with sea salt and fresh ground pepper. Transfer to a shallow dish and chill covered overnight. Serve at room temperature sprinkled with the almonds.

Carrot Pâté

Makes a 9 x 13 inch pan

This is a really versatile and yummy vegetable pâté. Serve with crackers or breadsticks or as a filling for pitas and sandwiches. This recipe makes a large amount which freezes really well wrapped in waxed paper and then foil.

2 cups	sunflower seeds		2 tbsp	dried thyme
4-5	large carrots, grated		½ cup	tamari
2 cloves	garlic, chopped		½ cup	sunflower oil
3	medium onions, chopped		½ cup	water
1 cup	whole wheat flour		1	lemon, juiced
1 cup	nutritional yeast		¼ cup	sesame seeds
2 tbsp	dried basil			

Lightly oil pan and shake sesame seeds to coat bottom and sides. Preheat oven to 300°.

In a food processor, grind the sunflower seeds, add carrots, garlic and onion, pulse to mince.

Combine flour, yeast and dry spices together in a small bowl. Add to the food processor along with tamari, water, sunflower oil and lemon juice. Pulse until well combined.

Spread into the prepared pan and bake 45 to 60 minutes until browned. Allow to cool. Cut into sections and serve.

Miso Dip & Baguette

Serves 2

This is a super dip. It is simple, savoury, quick and highly nutritious. We often have this in winter as a late night snack.

½ cup	tahini
⅓ cup	red miso
	fresh baguette or crackers
	sesame seeds

Slice the baguette into ½ inch slices. For 2 people you will need about 3 slices each. Toast lightly and keep warm. If desired sprinkle with a smidge of olive oil.

In a very small saucepan, over medium heat, cook tahini, stirring continuously. It will bubble while it's cooking. Remove from heat, wait 10 seconds for tahini to cool slightly and add miso, blending to form a thick paste. Sprinkle with the sesame seeds if you want to be fancy.

Serve warm with baguette.

White Bean Dip

Makes 2 cups

I love bean dips for their versatility, convenience, nutrition and flavour. Using roasted garlic adds depth and richness, but regular garlic works well and imparts a completely different flavour. Omit the sage/thyme/tarragon if you prefer.

2 cups	cooked white kidney beans (one 19 oz can)
1 head	garlic, roasted or 2 to 3 garlic cloves, minced
Juice	of half a lemon
¼ cup	pine nuts, toasted
¼ cup	fresh sage, thyme or tarragon, minced
1½ tsp	sea salt
½ tsp	white pepper
¼ cup	olive oil

Preheat oven to 425°.

Slice top off garlic, place on foil, sprinkle with salt, pepper and a touch of olive oil. Place in oven and bake for approximately 40 minutes. Let cool and remove garlic cloves.

Purée all ingredients in a food processor. Taste and adjust seasonings.

Hummus & Hummus

Makes 2 cups

" I couldn't leave this out of my book even though hummus can be found everywhere. It is a staple food to me. We eat it in pitas, on the side with vegetables, with falafels and as a snack throughout the day. It is nutritious and tasty. I have included two versions, classic and roasted red pepper. I use dried beans because I use the cooking water in the recipe. Alternatively use canned beans and water. "

Classic

2 cups	cooked chickpeas, reserve ¼ cup cooking water	2 tbsp	olive oil
2-3	large garlic cloves	¼ tsp	tobasco sauce or cayenne pepper
3 tbsp	lemon juice		sea salt to taste
¼ cup	tahini		parsley for garnish

Optional Additions:

1 tsp   cumin powder & 3 tbsp chopped cilantro
¼ cup   diced green onions, ¼ cup minced red pepper
½ tsp   paprika
¼ cup   toasted sesame seeds

Purée all ingredients in a blender until smooth and creamy, adding more liquid if necessary. Taste and adjust seasonings.

Roasted Red Pepper Version

2   red peppers, roasted
2 tsp   cumin seeds, toasted
3 tbsp   fresh cilantro, chopped

To the classic recipe, decrease tahini by one tablespoon, omit parsley, add peppers, cumin and cilantro and purée until creamy.

Flavoured Vinegars

Makes 2 cups

Home-made vinegars are in a class all their own and are very easy to make. They are an excellent way to capture the abundance of the seasons.

Strawberry Vinegar

1 pint	fresh Ontario strawberries, hulled and sliced
2 cups	white wine vinegar
2 tbsp	honey

In a bowl, gently stir together the strawberries, vinegar and honey. Let stand, covered at room temperature for 2 days. Discard strawberries and strain the vinegar into a bowl through a fine sieve that has been lined with cheesecloth. Transfer the vinegar to a sterilized bottle with a tight fitting lid and keep in a cool, dark place.

Tarragon Vinegar

1 bunch	fresh cut leafy tarragon
4 large	garlic cloves, peeled
1 tbsp	whole white peppercorns
4 cups	white wine vinegar

Use 2 mason jars or sterilized wine bottles. Divide recipe in half, placing several stalks tarragon, 2 cloves garlic, ½ tbsp peppercorns and 2 cups white wine vinegar into each bottle. Close lid tightly and store for 2 months in a cool, dark place. Vinegar keeps indefinitely.

Nayo ~ Mayo's

"Mayonnaise is very similar to aioli. Both are raw egg yolk based with a combination of spices, lemon, mustard, and sometimes vinegar. I make my own aioli when I have time. A faster method is to use prepared mayonnaise or for a soy based, non-egg version, use nayonnaise. I use these as spreads for baguettes, with grilled vegetables, as dips for sweet potato fries or with burgers. Use a good quality mayo or nayo for the following recipes."

Chipotle Mayo

Chipotle peppers have a hot, smoky flavour. They are sold in small cans mixed with Adobo sauce and can be found in most supermarkets.

1½ cups	mayonnaise
2 tsp	puréed chipotle peppers
1½ tsp	ground cumin
	sea salt to taste

Blend all ingredients in the food processor. Store in the refrigerator until serving. Keeps well for about a week.

Horseradish Mayo

Nice and spicy hot which pairs well with burgers or tempeh.

1 cup	mayonnaise
3 tbsp	fresh horseradish, grated or
2 tbsp	bottled, drained
½ tsp	tobasco

Blend together in a small bowl with a touch of salt, adding more horseradish if you like it spicier.

Tomato Mayo

¼ cup	red onion, minced
¼ cup	red pepper, minced
1 tbsp	sunflower oil
½ cup	tomato purée
2 cups	mayonnaise

In a small saucepan, cook the onion and red pepper in the oil until softened. Add the tomato purée and cook until all liquid is gone. Let cool then mix with the mayo. Add salt and pepper to taste.

Pesto Mayo

Substitute sundried tomato pesto for a different taste sensation.

1½ cups	mayonnaise
½ cup	pesto sauce, homemade or store bought

Blend together and add additional pesto if needed.

Tarragon Lime Mayo

1½ cups	mayonnaise
½ tsp	lime zest
2 tbsp	fresh tarragon, minced
1 tbsp	tarragon vinegar

Blend together in food processor until well combined. Add sea salt if desired.

Raita Three Ways

Serves 4

Raitas are yoghurt based Indian dishes served as accompaniments to curries. Yoghurt is usually mixed with a combination of fruits, vegetables and herbs. They are meant to be a cooling contrast to the heat of the curry.

Mixed Vegetable Raita

1½ cups	plain yoghurt	¼ tsp	sea salt
½ cup	orange pepper, diced	¼ tsp	fresh ground pepper
2	tomatoes, seeded & diced	½ whole	cucumber, peeled,
1 tsp	cumin seeds, toasted		diced
1 tbsp	coriander, minced		

Combine all ingredients in a bowl and mix thoroughly. Chill before serving.

Apple & Pear Raita

2 cups	plain yoghurt	½ tsp	cumin seeds, toasted
1 cup	granny smith apple	½ tsp	fennel seeds, toasted
1 cup	Bartlett pear	¼ tsp	sea salt
2 tsp	lemon juice		

Peel, core and dice apple and pear. Mix together with the lemon juice. Add yoghurt, seeds and sea salt to taste.

Mango Mint Raita

2 cups	plain yoghurt	1 tbsp	fresh mint, minced
2 cups	fresh mango, peeled, diced	½ tsp	fresh lime zest
1½ tsp	cumin seeds, toasted	¼ tsp	sea salt

Combine all ingredients together and serve.

Flavoured Butters

Orange Oregano ~ Lemon Herb ~ Basil Garlic

These are a wonderful addition to corn on the cob, muffins, scones, main dishes or anywhere you would use traditional butter. You can roll the butter as indicated or simply put into a festive bowl and serve. All butter should be at room temperature.

Orange Oregano

½ cup	unsalted butter		1 tbsp	fresh oregano, minced
1 tsp	orange zest		½ tsp	sea salt
1 tbsp	fresh chives, minced		¼ tsp	freshly ground pepper

Cream together all ingredients in a small bowl. Spoon butter in a line along a piece of foil and roll into a log. Refrigerate until hard. Remove from foil and slice into ¼ to ½ inch disks before serving.

Lemon Herb

1 cup	unsalted butter		½ tsp	dijon mustard
2 tsp	lemon juice		1	garlic clove, minced
1-2 tbsp	minced fresh herbs, parsley, chives, marjoram, or chervil		1 tsp	lemon zest

Proceed as in orange butter recipe.

Basil Garlic

¾ cup	unsalted butter
3 tbsp	fresh basil leaves, minced
1	garlic clove, minced

Proceed as in orange butter recipe.

Toasted Seeds

Toasted seeds add extra protein, flavour and a nice, crunchy texture to any dish. They are great on salads, sprinkled on soups, and as a nutritious afternoon or evening snack.

Savoury Sunflower Seeds

2 cups	sunflower seeds
2 tbsp	nutritional yeast
2 tsp	tamari or Braggs

Preheat oven to 350°. On a baking sheet, toast seeds until golden brown, approximately 12 minutes.

Combine all ingredients in a small bowl until covered. The seeds will steam and this is what cooks and binds the yeast to them. Let cool, stirring periodically so they don't stick. Store in a glass jar for up to 2 weeks.

Toasted Ponzu Seeds

1 cup	sunflower seeds
½ cup	pumpkin seeds
2 tsp	ponzu sauce, a citrus soy sauce
¼ tsp	lemon zest

Prepare as above, except once covered with sauce, put back in the oven on baking sheet for 10 minutes to bake the sauce into the seeds.

Toasted Garlic Seeds

1 cup	sunflower seeds	½ tsp	garlic powder
½ cup	pumpkin seeds	½ tsp	onion powder
2 tsp	Braggs		

Prepare as for ponzu seeds.

5

SOUPS
& STEWS

The Story of Granny's Calliloo Soup

This is a gift recipe, passed on to me from Granny (or Auntie Noo Noo as she is known to hundreds of people) after much prodding on my part. Her real name is Beryl and she's Andy's beloved mother who is, in her 90th year, still an incomparable chef and a force to be reckoned with in the kitchen. I absolutely adore her and it gives me great pleasure to watch her cook and then be the beneficiary of her efforts.

Born in Guyana in the West Indies, she has entertained royalty and cooking has been her passion all her life. She can recant recipes, formulas and techniques at the drop of a hat and the beauty of hearing her recipes is that there is always a story that goes with it; one that connects generations of people together. This is the magic of food and cooking, something that I believe is so lost in this day and age of packaged food. Cooking is about family, about community, about love for the earth and people.

I have written this recipe as it was told to me over a glass of wine one January winter night. I have made it many times and of course it isn't up to Granny's standard but it does pass Andy's childrens' taste tests.

Granny lovingly obliges, as best she can, all requests for favourite items, especially from her grandchildren. Her other fans include the President of Guyana, who has one of her Christmas Black cakes shipped to him every year. It is out of this world. However, Calliloo Soup is the only recipe of hers I am allowed to put in my book. (The Black cake recipe is locked in my secret vault, along with other gems that have been entrusted to me.)

Calliloo is a broad leaf spinach found in the West Indies. It is difficult to find here but regular spinach is what we use as a fine substitute. It is a hearty, thick soup that you can serve on its own or with crab legs or dumplings. So enjoy – it makes a huge amount, enough to serve 15 people. It freezes really well so you can have it on hand whenever you crave it.

Granny's Calliloo Soup

Serves 15

2 pkgs	frozen spinach	2 tbsp	dried thyme
2 pkgs	frozen okra	1 bunch	Italian parsley, chopped
3 or 4	onions, chopped	2 tbsp	olive oil
5 - 6	celery stalks chopped		water or vegetable stock
6	wiri peppers		

Optional: ½ lb crab meat or a small whole crab

Wiri peppers are rare Guyanese peppers that are small, round and bead-like, red or yellow in colour, with a wonderful, aromatic flavour. You won't be able to find these, I only include them because they are part of the original recipe. If you want more heat add a touch of cayenne to the final product.

In a large stock pot, over medium heat, simmer spinach, okra, celery and onions about 45 minutes. Purée. Add thyme, salt and pepper to taste and Italian parsley.

Add water or vegetable stock to cover. Add more liquid if you want a thinner soup.

If using crab meat, first stir fry it with a few chopped onions, garlic and pepper, then add to the soup, stirring to combine.

Granny's Dumplings:

2 scoops	flour (1½ cups)	½ tsp	sea salt
2 tsp	baking powder	2 tbsp	unsalted butter
½ tsp	organic sugar		ice water

Combine dry ingredients, add butter and ice water, one tablespoon at a time until mixture can be formed into small balls. Drop onto surface of soup, partially cover, allowing the steam from the soup to cook dumplings, about 20 minutes.

Easy Soup Preparation

First ~ Stock

In all of my soups you can use either water or stock but my preference is stock. Simply put, it is the essence of vegetables cooked in water. Scraps, shavings, a few herbs in a bouquet garni, and you have a stock. (Whenever you are cooking, save time by freezing scraps, remove from bag and drop into soup.) They should take no more than an hour to prepare. You don't need to stir the pot while they are cooking; just throw your vegetables into a large pot, add water, (about 2 to 3 inches above the vegetables), bring to a boil and simmer.

When using vegetables for stock preparation, the amount and type of vegetable will influence the final outcome of your soup. For example, using beets in corn stock will change the colour to off-red.

Vegetables you can use in stock are: corn cobs, mushroom stems, leeks, garlic, scallions, parsnips, squash, carrots, fennel, celery leaves, parsley leaves and thyme leaves. Avoid cabbage, asparagus, beets, and too much onion. They will overpower your soup.

Bouquet garnis are herbs in a cheesecloth bag dropped into the soup. The choice of herbs will depend on the soup you are making. Parsley, bay leaves, fennel seeds, cumin seeds, peppercorns, anise, and cinnamon are just a few examples.

Second ~ Adding Depth

Start with onions, garlic and celery. Add herbs and a touch of salt and pepper. Next, add vegetables and stock. You are now layering your soup and creating depth of flavour. It is important to taste along the way to enhance the basic flavours you are creating.

Bring out the flavours with lemon, wine, vinegar, beer, hot sauce, miso, tamarind, maple syrup, honey, yoghurt and cream. Taste and finally garnish with herbs, croutons, fried onions, fried mushrooms, or roasted peppers.

Basic & Roasted Vegetable Stock

Basic Stock

4 cups	mixed vegetable shavings, carrots, fennel, celery, celeriac, garlic cloves, onion, broccoli & cauliflower stalks, corn cobs
1 bouquet garni	depending on the soup you are preparing, use a combination of summer savoury, oregano, basil, thyme, fennel, 10 peppercorns, 5 bay leaves, parsley, dill or coriander sprigs
Water	to cover by 2 to 3 inches

Put everything into a large pot with water, bring to a boil and simmer over low heat for about an hour. Remove from heat and strain and discard vegetables.

Roasted Vegetable Stock

For a heartier stock use roasted vegetables. Roasting caramelizes and sweetens the vegetables creating a deeply flavoured stock.

8 cups	mixed whole vegetables for roasting such as carrots, butternut squash, parsnip, fennel, red onion, garlic cloves, sweet potatoes

olive oil
sea salt and pepper
water

Preheat oven to 350°. Toss all vegetables in a bowl with a little oil to cover. Add salt and pepper and roast until very tender. Remove, let cool and purée in a food processor.

Place puréed vegetables in a large pot with water to cover by 2 to 3 inches, stirring to combine. Bring to a boil and simmer for an hour until ready to use. If too thick add more water.

Miso Soup

Serves 4-5

"Miso soup is one of the most nurturing of all soups. Miso is a soy product full of live enzymes and nutrients. It is important to add it at the end of cooking and never to boiling water, which will kill the enzymes. This recipe is a little elaborate but you can simply put a tablespoon of miso in hot water for a healing broth. Serve for breakfast, lunch or dinner. It is always a welcome addition to a meal."

3	garlic cloves, minced		¼ cup	miso, dark or light
2 tbsp	ginger, peeled & minced		1 tbsp	umeboshi paste
2 tbsp	toasted sesame oil		½ cup	diced, soft tofu
½ cup	carrots, julienned		¼ cup	tamari
½ cup	daikon, julienned		8 inch	piece Kombu
1 cup	kale or spinach, shredded		5 cups	water

Optional: mung bean sprouts, diced green onions, red pepper shreds

In a large pot, bring water to a boil with kombu, add tamari.

Sauté garlic and ginger in the sesame oil, over medium high heat until fragrant and golden, add to the soup broth.

Remove kombu, add vegetables and tofu. Cook gently over medium to low heat for approximately 10 minutes.

Remove 1 cup of broth from soup and mix with miso and umeboshi paste in a small bowl until smooth, add back to the soup. Do not let the soup boil, adjust seasonings and serve hot.

Lentil Soup

Serves 6

This is a light lentil soup with a burst of flavour from the lemon juice and dill. Vitamin packed kale or swiss chard makes this a must in the winter months. Serve with foccacia bread and organic greens.

2 tbsp	sunflower oil	5 cups	basic stock
2 cups	onions, chopped	2	bay leaves
3 tbsp	garlic, minced	1 tsp	sea salt
2 cups	carrots, diced	½ tsp	fresh ground pepper
1 cup	sweet potato, diced	2 tbsp	fresh dill, chopped
1 cup	butternut squash, diced	¼ cup	lemon juice
2	stalks celery, diced	3 cups	kale or swiss chard, shredded
1 cup	red lentils		

Rinse the lentils in several changes of water until it runs clear.

In a large pot over medium high heat, sauté the onions, garlic, carrots, sweet potatoes and squash. Add salt and cook until the vegetables soften. Add the lentils and celery and continue to cook another 5 minutes. Add stock or water, bay leaves and reduce heat to low. Cover and simmer until vegetables are tender and the lentils are creamy.

Remove from heat and stir in the lemon, dill and greens. Cover and let the heat from the soup steam the greens. Season with salt and pepper and serve immediately.

CHEF'S TIP:

It is important to pick over the lentils and wash in several changes of water. They can contain pebbles and dirt and are covered in white talc to preserve and prevent sticking…yucky.

Spring Minestrone Soup

Serves 8-12

> "My approach to soup is to throw whatever I have on hand into the pot. Trust your instincts. This is called spring minestrone because that is when it was created. It is packed full of flavour and vitamins. The leafy greens can be spinach, swiss chard, kale or a combination of all three. If you add the tomatoes, it becomes a more classical minestrone. If you omit them, it becomes a beautiful, green, spring soup."

12 cups	basic stock (approx.)	3 cups	zucchini, cubed
3 tbsp	olive oil	3 cups	cabbage, shredded
2 cups	yellow onions, chopped	3 cups	green beans
2	leeks, white part, chopped	2 cups	peas, fresh or frozen
6	garlic cloves, minced	1 can	white kidney beans
3	stalks celery, chopped	6 cups	leafy greens
3	carrots, chopped	3	bay leaves
2	potatoes, chopped	½ cup	very small pasta

Optional: 1 – 28 oz can chopped tomatoes and 2 tbsp tomato paste

Herbs

1 tsp	oregano	1 tsp	sage
2 tsp	fennel seed, toasted	1 tsp	sea salt
2 tsp	dried thyme	1 tsp	fresh ground pepper

In a large pot over medium heat, cook onions, leeks, garlic and celery until just soft. Add herbs and rest of vegetables except white beans and leafy greens. Cook 5 minutes, add stock to cover. Bring to a boil, reduce heat and cook 15 minutes until vegetables are al dente (still a bit firm). Add white beans and pasta, tomatoes, tomato paste if using. Simmer for half an hour then add greens. Let sit 15 minutes until serving. As with most soups, the flavours improve the next day.

Summer Corn Chowder

Serves 8

This is perfect in late summer when Ontario corn is ripe for the picking. Making the stock with the corn cobs takes this chowder to a whole other level.

Stock

4	cobs corn, corn removed & reserved for soup	10	whole peppercorns
1 large	white onion, quartered	3 bay	leaves
2	cloves garlic	1 tsp	sea salt
	sprigs of parsley, tarragon & basil	8 cups	water

Soup

1 tbsp	olive oil	1 tsp	each sea salt & pepper
1 tbsp	unsalted butter	2 cups	red pepper, diced
2 large	onions, chopped	8 cups	corn stock
4	garlic cloves, minced	1-28 oz	can fire roasted tomatoes
4	stalks celery, chopped	1 cup	cream, milk or soy milk
2	jalapeno peppers, minced	½ cup	mixed herbs, tarragon, basil, marjoram, oregano
3	red potatoes, cubed		
½ cup	each, peeled carrot & butternut squash, cubed	4 cups	reserved corn juice of one lime

To Make Stock

Put everything into a large stock pot, bring to a boil and let simmer for 1 hour. Remove from heat and strain. Set aside.

To Make Soup

In a large soup pot over medium heat, cook onions, garlic, jalapenos and celery in the oil and butter until softened. Add potatoes, corn, carrots, squash, salt, pepper and cook for 2 minutes. Add stock to cover, red peppers and tomatoes, cook over low heat for 20 minutes until vegetables are tender. Add cream and herbs and continue to cook without boiling for 10 minutes. Add lime juice, adjust seasonings.

Curried Sweet Potato Soup

Serves 8-10

This is a lovely Thai inspired soup. Sweet potatoes are packed full of antioxidants and ginger is a natural blood detoxifier. This is perfect for entertaining guests or for everyday. Add sambal oelek, an Indonesian spicy red pepper sauce, for extra heat.

2 tbsp	sunflower oil	2	granny smith apples, peeled & chopped
1 tbsp	unsalted butter		
1	onion, chopped	6 cups	basic stock
1 cup	leeks, white part, chopped	1 cup	coconut milk
2 stalks	celery, chopped	½ tsp	each sea salt & pepper
3 tbsp	ginger root, minced	2 tbsp	lime juice
2 tsp	curry paste or powder	1 tsp	lime zest
6 cups	sweet potatoes, chopped	2 tbsp	fresh coriander, minced
1 cup	red potatoes, chopped		

Optional: 1 tsp sambal oelek

In a large stock pot over medium low heat, cook the onion, leeks, celery and ginger root in the oil and butter until soft. Add the curry paste and cook one minute.

Add potatoes and apples, cook for 5 minutes stirring frequently. Add stock and simmer until the vegetables soften about 20 minutes. Add the coconut milk, lime juice and zest and cook another 5 minutes without boiling. Remove from heat and using an immersion blender or food processor purée until completely smooth.

Return to heat, add salt and pepper, extra lime zest if you want, and garnish with coriander.

Wild Salmon Chowder

Serves 2

This is a rich soup, perfect for entertaining. It is hearty and can stand alone at the dinner table with fresh, warm, crusty bread. The recipe easily doubles and triples, adjust the spices accordingly.

½ lb	sweet potatoes, peeled cut into ¼ inch cubes		½ lb	wild salmon fillets, skinned
1 tbsp	lemon juice		1 tbsp	flour
½ tsp	sea salt		2 oz	smoked salmon, chopped
¼ tsp	white pepper, to taste		2 tbsp	fresh dill, chopped
2½ cups	milk or soy milk		2 tbsp	unsalted butter
¾ cup	minced onion			

In a small pot, combine potatoes, ¼ tsp salt and the milk. Bring to a low boil, turn heat down and simmer for about 10 minutes until the potatoes are almost tender.

In another saucepan, over medium low heat, cook onion in the butter until softened. Place the salmon steak on the onion, and sprinkle with remaining salt, white pepper and lemon juice. Cover and cook the salmon turning once for about 8 to 10 minutes or until it is still firm, transfer salmon to a plate.

Sprinkle the flour over the onion and cook over medium low heat, stirring, for about 3 minutes. Add the milk mixture, stirring occasionally for 5 minutes. Add the salmon steak (breaking it into chunks), the smoked salmon, dill, extra white pepper and salt to taste. Continue to cook until heated through. Do not boil. Garnish with dill sprigs.

Carrot Ginger Bisque

Serves 6-8

This soup is a must during the winter months. Vibrant orange in colour and filled with antioxidants and vitamins, it promotes good health.

2 tbsp	unsalted butter		2 lbs	organic carrots, chopped
1 tbsp	olive oil		3 tbsp	grated ginger, or to taste
1 large	onion, chopped		3 cups	basic stock (approx.)
1	leek, white part, chopped		1 can	coconut milk
5	garlic cloves, minced			
	sea salt & white pepper to taste			

Optional:

1 tsp	sambal oelek, or to taste
2 tsp	lemon juice

In a large pot over medium heat, add butter and oil. Add onion and leeks, cooking until tender. Add garlic, carrots, ginger, salt and pepper, cook another couple of minutes. Add stock to cover and simmer until soft.

Purée the vegetables with an immersion blender. Add coconut milk and simmer on low (do not boil), until ready to serve. Adjust seasonings, add sambal oelek and lemon juice if desired.

Parsnip Squash Bisque

Serves 6-8

Parsnips are powerful and full flavoured autumn vegetables. They make an excellent addition to soups and stews. They can be roasted or made into yummy chips for snacking. Adding the tofu makes the soup creamy and rich, but it isn't necessary for flavour.

1	onion, chopped	1 tsp	dried dill
1 large	leek, white part, chopped	8 cups	basic vegetable stock
4 large	carrots, chopped	½ cup	organic oats, ground
4 large	parsnips, chopped	2 tsp	sea salt
1 small	acorn squash, chopped	¼ tsp	white pepper
2 tbsp	sunflower oil	¼ cup	fresh dill, chopped
1 tsp	dried thyme	1 pkg	silken tofu, crumbled

Optional: 3 tsp umeboshi vinegar or lemon juice

Peel and chop all vegetables. In a large pot over medium heat, sauté onion and leeks in oil until transparent. Add vegetables and herbs and continue to cook for about 5 minutes.

Add stock, oats, salt and pepper. Bring to a boil and simmer for about 30 minutes. Add fresh dill, tofu and vinegar. Using an immersion blender, purée the soup until creamy. Adjust seasonings and serve.

CHEF'S TIP:

Umeboshi vinegar is made from the juice left from pickling umeboshi plums. It is good for indigestion and helps to balance dishes containing grains or starches. It is both salty and tart.

Shrimp Bisque

Serves 10

This is a rich and elegant soup that is perfect for dinner parties. Garnish with sautéed baby shrimp if desired.

3 tbsp	olive oil		2 cups	basic stock
1½ lbs	medium shrimp		1 cup	dry white wine
¼ cup	unsalted butter		1	bay leaf
1 cup	shallots, diced		1 tsp	sea salt
1 large	carrot, chopped		¼ tsp	cayenne pepper
1 large	celery stalk, chopped		2 cups	diced tomatoes
1 cup	potato, chopped		2 cups	cream or soy milk

Shell and devein the shrimp, reserve shells.

In a large stock pot over medium high heat, add olive oil and cook shrimp shells, stirring until they turn pink. Discard shells leaving oil in pot.

Add shrimp to oil and cook over medium heat until they turn pink. Remove with a slotted spoon and set aside.

Add butter to pot, and cook shallots, carrot, celery and potato, stirring until they are slightly tender. Stir in the stock, wine, bay leaf, salt and cayenne. Bring to a boil, reduce heat to a low simmer and cook another 15 minutes until vegetables are tender and flavours develop. Remove bay leaf, add tomatoes and shrimp and using an immersion blender, purée until smooth. Stir in cream or soy milk and heat until hot. Do not boil. Adjust seasonings if necessary.

Wild Mushroom Bisque

Serves 6-8

Andy's beautiful daughters, Shu Wen, Hana, and Shu Wei are always requesting a mushroom soup on their visits to Harmony Dawn. This is one of many that I have on hand for them when they come to visit. Choose any combination of mushrooms.

2 lbs	assorted mushrooms, portobello, chanterelle, morels, oyster, button
½ cup	unsalted butter
2 tsp	lemon juice, or to taste
1 large	onion, chopped
2 cloves	garlic, minced
½ cup	all-purpose flour
6 cups	basic stock
2 tsp	sea salt
½ tsp	white pepper
¼ cup	cooking sherry
1 cup	cream or soy milk

Trim mushrooms and remove stems, set aside. Slice mushrooms thinly. In a large pot over medium heat, add ¼ cup butter, mushrooms and lemon juice and cook until mushrooms are just tender. Remove mushrooms from pot and set aside.

Reduce heat to medium low, add remaining butter and cook onion, garlic and stems until tender. Stir in flour until blended and cook for about 1 minute, stirring constantly. Stir in stock slowly and cook until mixture is thickened.

Return mushrooms to pot. Purée, using an immersion blender. Add sherry, cream, salt and pepper. Simmer until heated through. Do not boil.

Spicy Peanut Soup with Lentils

Serves 10

This soup is fun and full of crunch and flavour. Add more peanut butter if you like a thicker soup. Kaffir lime leaves can be found in Asian markets. They have a lovely lime, curry flavour. Buy them and freeze until you need to use them. If you can't find them, substitute lime juice to taste.

2 tsp	each, fennel, cumin & coriander seeds	3 tsp	fresh ginger, minced
		1 tsp	dried chilies
¼ cup	peanut oil	5 cups	basic stock or water
3 med.	carrots, diced	3 cups	coconut milk
3 med.	red onions, thinly sliced	6	kaffir lime leaves
1 large	leek, white part, thinly sliced	¾ cup	red lentils
1 cup	corn	½ cup	organic peanut butter
4	garlic cloves, minced		

Garnish: ½ cup diced red pepper, ½ cup chopped coriander & toasted unsalted peanuts, coarsely chopped

Toast the seeds for 2 minutes until fragrant. Let cool, then grind. Wash lentils in several changes of water until it runs clear.

Heat oil over medium high heat, cook carrots, onion, leek, garlic, ginger and chilies until tender. Add ground spices, stirring for a minute or two.

Add the stock or water, coconut milk, corn and lime leaves and bring to a low boil. Stir in the lentils and simmer over low heat until tender, about 25 minutes. Mix the peanut butter with ½ cup of water and add to the soup. You may need to add a bit more water to the soup if it is too thick. Garnish and serve.

Lentil Dhal

Serves 5-7

" In India, dhal is a staple food, eaten for breakfast, lunch, or dinner. It is satisfying, nutritious and really simple to prepare. Dhal is made with lentils or split peas and combinations of spices that vary from one region in India to another. This is one of our personal favourites. We make a large batch and freeze it in small quantities to have on hand. Garam masala is a blend of spices from northern India. "

2½ cups	red lentils	¾ tsp	mustard seeds, toasted
2 tsp	turmeric	½ tsp	cinnamon
2 tbsp	sunflower oil	1 tsp	cayenne pepper
1½ cups	onions, chopped	½ cup	lemon juice (approx.)
4 large	garlic cloves, minced	2 cups	canned, diced tomatoes
3 tsp	curry powder	3 cups	chopped kale
3 tsp	cumin seeds, toasted	½ cup	coriander, chopped
1 tsp	garam masala		sea salt to taste
1 tsp	dried chilies		fresh pepper to taste
1½ tsp	coriander seeds, toasted		

Rinse the lentils in several changes of water until the water runs clear. Place lentils and turmeric in a large pot with enough water to cover by an inch and a half. Bring to a boil and simmer for approximately 30 minutes, removing white film that appears during cooking.

Meanwhile heat oil in skillet, add onions and garlic and sauté until tender. Add all the spices and cook for another minute or two.

Whisk lentils until creamy and smooth. Add onion mixture, lemon juice and tomatoes, simmer over low heat for 30 minutes. About 20 minutes before serving, add greens. The flavour improves over time.

Adzuki Bean Stew

Serves 4

Adzukis are protein packed alkaline beans that are easy to digest. Serve over brown rice with a sprinkling of dulse for a macrobiotic feast. I use dried beans that I soak overnight and then cook, but canned beans work well in this recipe.

2 tbsp	sunflower oil	1 cup	dried hijiki
1 large	onion, sliced in slivers	½ cup	tamari
2 cups	carrots, sliced in chunks	½ cup	shiitake cooking water
2 cups	dried shiitakes	3 cups	kale, shredded
4 cups	cooked adzuki beans	3 tbsp	dark miso

Place shiitakes in a saucepan covered with water and bring to a boil, reduce heat and simmer for 15 minutes. Turn off heat, cover and let sit for 15 minutes. Remove shiitakes and slice, removing hard stems and reserving cooking water.

In a small bowl, cover hijiki with cold water for 5 minutes. Remove and set aside.

In a large skillet over medium high heat, sauté onions and carrots in the oil for 2 to 3 minutes until just tender. Add adzukis, shiitakes, hijiki and tamari. Add shiitake water if dish needs more gravy. Cook for 5 minutes, add kale, cover and cook until bright green. In a small bowl combine miso with a little shiitake water to make a smooth paste.

Remove stew from heat and stir in miso. Serve immediately.

Roasted Tempeh & Acorn Squash Stew

Serves 5

This dish is very popular at Harmony Dawn. It is savoury, simple and relatively yang, ideal for autumn and winter. Serve over organic brown rice with a side of steamed cauliflower and sesame tahini sauce (pg.102).

1 pkg	tempeh, plain	2 tbsp	sesame seeds, toasted
1 small	acorn squash	½ cup	tamari
10	cooked shiitake mushrooms, reserving water, (pg.150)	¼ cup	green onions, cut in slivers
	sunflower oil		

Preheat oven to 400°. Cut tempeh into ½ inch cubes. In a small bowl marinate tempeh with 1 tablespoon tamari. Place on a lightly oiled baking sheet and bake, turning once for about 20 minutes or until brown and crispy.

While the tempeh is baking, peel the squash, cut in half, remove seeds and cut into 1 inch cubes. Steam until al dente (still a bit firm). Remove from pot and set aside.

In a large heavy pot over moderately high heat, sauté green onions and sesame seeds in 2 tbsp sunflower oil. Add 2 tbsp tamari and let simmer 2 minutes. Add the tempeh, shiitakes and another 2 tbsp tamari and simmer another minute. Put in the reserved acorn squash and stir gently, being careful not to break the squash. Finally, stir in remaining tamari and approximately ½ cup of the reserved shiitake water. Simmer until hot and garnish with additional sesame seeds and green onions.

Before serving, adjust seasonings, adding more shiitake water and tamari to create a savoury gravy.

Cauliflower Stew with Lentils

Serves 4

This is a simple and hearty stew, boosted with the protein of lentils and the vitamins of cauliflower and carrots.

4 tbsp	sunflower oil	1 head	cauliflower, cut into florets
1 cup	onions, chopped	1	red bell pepper, chopped
2 large	carrots, chopped	3 cups	basic stock or water
2 cloves	garlic, minced	2	bay leaves
2 tbsp	Italian parsley, chopped	½ tsp	chili powder
1½ cups	green or brown lentils	1 tsp	cumin
1-28 oz	can, chopped tomatoes	¼ tsp	cayenne pepper

Wash lentils in several changes of water until it runs clear.

Heat oil in a large saucepan, add onions and garlic and sauté over medium heat for 5 minutes. Add the lentils, carrots, spices and the stock. Bring to a boil and simmer over low heat for 20 to 30 minutes. Add tomatoes, cauliflower and bell pepper, cook for another 10 minutes. Before serving add parsley.

Serve over rice or as a thick soup with bread.

Nicola's Cioppino

Serves 2-4

" Cioppino is a hearty fish soup or stew, made with a tomato base. You can put as much different seafood in as you like. My version is simplified and super fast. Preparation and cooking should take no more than 25 minutes. It's elegant enough to serve at dinner parties or during the week over brown rice or with crusty bread. "

2 tbsp	unsalted butter		1 lb	medium shrimps
2 tbsp	olive oil		1 large	yellow pepper, cut into thick strips
2	garlic cloves, chopped			
1	golden onion, sliced		1	bay leaf
1 cup	dry white wine		1 tsp	dried oregano
3 cups	canned, chopped tomatoes		1 tsp	dried basil
1 lb	halibut or haddock cut into 1 inch cubes		½ cup	Italian parsley, chopped sea salt & fresh pepper

Optional: 1 cup cooked, diced potatoes & 2 tbsp lemon juice
1 cup chopped Kalamata olives

In a large skillet over medium high heat melt the butter and oil. Add garlic and onion and cook for about 3 minutes. Stir in tomatoes, wine, herbs, yellow pepper, bay leaf and any optional ingredients. Simmer for about 15 minutes.

Add halibut/haddock and shrimp to pan and simmer for about 5 minutes, until cooked through. Taste, add salt, pepper and parsley. Serve hot.

6
ENTRÉES

Purple Cabbage over Buckwheat Noodles

Serves 4

> This dish promotes great health. It is macrobiotic, easy to digest and the combination of ingredients have an alkalizing effect on your body, creating balance. Cabbage and turmeric are must have cancer fighters. Dulse is a sea vegetable that is extremely high in protein, iron, B6, B12 and other nutrients. Buckwheat contains all 8 amino acids, calcium, vitamin E and B complex vitamins. Yummy!

2 tbsp	olive oil	½ cup	tahini
¾	small purple cabbage, thickly sliced	½ cup	tamari
		¼ cup	water or soy milk
2 large	leeks, white part only, sliced	1 pkg	firm tofu, cubed
		¼ cup	dulse
1 tsp	dried chilies	1½ pkgs	buckwheat noodles, cooked
2 tsp	turmeric		

In a large skillet over medium high heat, cook leeks in the olive oil until softened. Add cabbage, chilies and turmeric, cooking until cabbage has softened. Turn heat down to medium low and add tahini and tamari, blending until combined thoroughly. Add tofu and simmer, adding more water if sauce becomes too thick. Add 2 tbsp dulse and combine.

While the cabbage mixture simmers, bring a large pot of salted water to the boil. Add the noodles and cook according to package directions (they cook very fast).

To serve, combine the noodles and cabbage together in bowls and garnish with remaining dulse.

Spicy Shrimp with Lemon Spaghetti

Serves 4

The lemon pasta accentuates the spiciness of the shrimp. I use kamut spaghetti but any whole grain pasta will work.

Pasta Sauce

1 tbsp	unsalted butter	½ tsp	dried chilies
½ tbsp	olive oil	2 cups	chopped tomatoes
1 lb	medium sized shrimp, peeled	1 cup	dry white wine
		1 tsp	dried oregano
1	medium onion, sliced	1 tsp	sea salt

Spaghetti Sauce

1 pkg	kamut spaghetti	⅔ cup	freshly grated Parmesan
⅔ cup	olive oil	1 tsp	lemon zest
½ cup	lemon juice	2 tbsp	chopped fresh basil

Cook the spaghetti in boiling, salted water, until al dente (still a bit firm) or approximately 8 minutes. Drain, reserving ½ cup of cooking water.

To make the pasta sauce, season shrimp with ¼ tsp salt and the chilies. In a skillet over medium high heat, sauté shrimp in the olive oil and butter until just cooked. Remove from pan and set aside. In the same pan cook onion with ¼ tsp salt until translucent. Add wine, oregano and tomatoes and cook until reduced by half (it should be quite thick). Add shrimp and cook an additional minute.

In a separate bowl, mix all spaghetti sauce ingredients together, except garnish and toss with the cooked pasta, adding a smidge of the pasta water if needed.

To Serve

On a large platter, place the lemon spaghetti and top with the shrimp sauce. Garnish with the basil and extra lemon zest.

Stinky Pasta

Serves 4

> "We affectionately call this dish "stinky pasta" in our family. We could have called it "fresh tomato and basil pasta with garlic" but for some reason the "stinky" has stuck. In August when tomatoes are abundant and basil is at its peak, we just can't get enough of it. Add grilled shrimps for a non–veg option."

1 pkg.	kamut spaghetti	1 tsp	sea salt
8–10	plum tomatoes, chopped	1 tsp	freshly ground pepper
1 large	bunch basil, chopped	½ tsp	dried chilies
3 large	garlic cloves, minced	¼ cup	olive oil, plus 1 tbsp
2	anchovy fillets, minced, (omit if vegetarian)	½ cup	fresh grated Parmesan

In a large pot bring 8 cups of water to a boil. Add ½ tsp of salt, 1 tbsp of olive oil and boil the pasta until al dente (still a bit firm), about 8 minutes. Drain and keep warm.

Meanwhile, in a large bowl combine the tomatoes, basil, garlic, anchovies, salt, pepper, chilies and olive oil. Add the pasta and Parmesan cheese and combine thoroughly.

Serve garnished with fresh basil and extra Parmesan.

Noodles with Spicy Tofu Peanut Sauce

Serves 4

This is such a versatile dish. Serve over buckwheat noodles or black rice with a side of wilted beet and dandelion greens for contrast. Vegetarian worcestershire sauce and black sesame seeds are available at natural and health food stores. Always use organic peanut butter which has been freshly ground.

4 cups	cooked buckwheat noodles	⅓ cup	tamari
1 pkg	firm tofu, cut into chunks	4 tbsp	sesame oil
3 tbsp	peanut oil	2 tbsp	worcestershire sauce
2 tbsp	minced garlic	1 tsp	dried chilies
2 tbsp	minced ginger	½ cup	stock or hot water
1 cup	carrot, julienned	½ cup	coriander, chopped
1 cup	red pepper, julienned	½ cup	toasted cashews, coarsely chopped
¾ cup	chunky peanut butter		
1 cup	green onion, finely sliced	¼ cup	black sesame seeds

Cook the buckwheat noodles according to package directions, drain and set aside.

Heat oil in a large skillet or wok over medium heat. Add garlic, ginger, carrot and pepper, cook 30 seconds. Stir in peanut butter, ½ cup green onion, tamari, sesame oil, worcestershire sauce and 1 tsp of the chilies. Reduce heat to low and add water a little at a time until creamy. You may need to add more water. Add tofu and cook a couple of minutes until heated through. Taste sauce and adjust seasonings.

Mix sauce with noodles. Add coriander and remaining green onions, combining thoroughly. Garnish with cashews and sesame seeds.

Burger Basics

Burgers are very popular items on the Harmony Dawn menu. Consistently, the feedback I get from people is, "These can't be veggie burgers, they aren't dry and tasteless." Most veggie burgers on the market are packaged and/or frozen which tend to make them lackluster and tasteless.

The possible combinations are endless and I just love to experiment with different flavours and textures. They invariably have a grain, a bean, different vegetables done different ways, and herbs and spices. Although I have included several recipes in my book, the following basic rules will allow you to create your own unique burgers. Have fun!

1. Being too exact will work against you; trust your instincts. Use what you like, whether millet instead of rice or tofu instead of tempeh. Experiment with different herbs and spices as well.

2. Let the ingredients cool down before shaping. This allows the flavours to develop and makes the burgers easier to shape.

3. You can sauté or bake your burgers. The texture will be different depending on the technique. I tend to bake them because the outside will be crispy and the inside soft, without using excessive oil.

4. You can use breadcrumbs, oats, egg, or ground nuts to hold them together.

5. It is easier to shape the burgers if your hands are slightly wet. You may have to rinse your hands occasionally. Alternatively you can use clean latex gloves.

Burger Fixin's

Fixin's are considered by some as the best and most fun part of having a burger. Dress them up with salsa, flavoured aioli's, mayo's, nayo's, and of course the standard pickles, organic ketchup and mustards.

Fresh Tomato Salsa

3 cups	tomatoes, minced	½ tsp	dried chilies
½ cup	red onion, minced	¼ of	1 jalapeno, minced
¼ cup	green onion, minced		pinch sea salt &
¼ cup	Italian parsley, minced		fresh pepper

Combine all ingredients together and serve.

Horseradish Aioli

2 cups	mayo or nayo	½ tsp	lemon juice
4 tbsp	grated fresh horseradish		pinch sea salt &
			fresh pepper

Combine all ingredients together and serve.

Tarragon Lemon Lime Aioli

2 cups	mayo or nayo	1 tbsp	lemon juice
2 tsp	lemon zest	½ tbsp	lime juice
1 tsp	lime zest	1 cup	tarragon, minced

Combine all ingredients together, add salt and pepper and serve.

Tartar Sauce

2 cups	mayo or nayo	1 tbsp	green onion, minced
1 tsp	lemon zest	1 tbsp	capers, chopped
1 tbsp	lemon juice	1 tbsp	chopped chives, parley
4-5	gherkins, minced		& tarragon

Combine as above.

Summer Vegetable & Tofu Burgers

Serves 6-8

These are fabulous and hearty all-vegetable burgers. Top with either tomato salsa or horseradish aioli (pg.161). Serve with homemade buns, fresh corn on the cob and a green salad.

2½ cups	cooked brown rice		1 cup	hazelnuts, toasted
2 cups	cooked sweet yams		1½ cups	organic oats
2 tbsp	sunflower oil		4 tbsp	nutritional yeast
1½ cups	carrots, grated		3 tbsp	tamari
2 cups	beets, grated		2 tbsp	dried dill
1½ cups	zucchini, grated		½ cup	Italian parsley, chopped
1 to 2	yellow onions, chopped		½ tsp	sea salt (or to taste)
3 large	garlic cloves, minced		1 tsp	ground pepper
1 cup	firm tofu, crumbled			

Mash yams and set aside. In a colander strain the beets and zucchini to remove excess liquid.

In a large skillet over medium heat, sauté onions, carrots, beets, zucchini, and garlic in the sunflower oil for 5 minutes.

In a large bowl combine all ingredients and mix thoroughly with a sturdy wooden spoon. Taste and adjust seasonings. Shape into patties and place on a lightly oiled baking sheet in a 350° oven for 30 minutes.

Shiitake Mushroom Burgers

Makes 10-12 large burgers

The shiitake mushrooms make a full flavoured "meaty" burger which is perfect in any season. Serve with stir-fried Asian greens and tahini sesame dressing (pg.102).

3 cups	dried shiitake mushrooms (enough for 4 cups cooked)	1 med.	red onion, chopped
		1 cup	oats
2 cups	cooked blacked rice	3 tbsp	tamari
2 cups	cooked yams, mashed	1 tbsp	miso
3 cups	fresh chanterelles & oyster mushrooms, chopped	½ tbsp	chilies
		5 green	onions, chopped
2 tbsp	toasted sesame oil	½ cup	coriander chopped
4 large	garlic cloves		sea salt & pepper
3 tbsp	ginger, minced		toasted sesame seeds

Place the shiitakes in a medium pot with enough water to cover by 2 inches. Bring to boil and simmer about 15 minutes. Turn off heat, cover and let sit for 15 minutes. Remove mushrooms and squeeze out excess water. Coarsely chop discarding hard stem. Set aside.

In a large skillet, heat the sesame oil for 30 seconds, add ginger and garlic and fast cook for 1 minute. Add onion and fresh mushrooms and cook for 5 minutes until most of the liquid has evaporated. Put mixture in a food processor with the shiitake mushrooms and pulse until coarsely chopped, but not minced.

In a large bowl, combine mushroom mixture, rice, yams and all remaining ingredients, mixing well. Taste and add salt and pepper and more tamari if desired. Let sit 1 hour to allow flavours to develop. Sprinkle with sesame seeds and place on a lightly, sesame oiled baking sheet and bake at 350° for about 30 minutes.

Salmon Yam Black Rice Burgers

Serves 5-7

These burgers are more than just burgers, they are a taste sensation. Serve with a roasted root vegetable platter and fig balsamic sauce (pg.116), organic green salad and sweet potato rolls (pg.30). Using canned wild salmon is convenient but my preference is to lightly poach a wild salmon fillet and then proceed with the recipe.

3 to 4	yams, peeled & cut into ½ inch dice (about 2 cups)	¼ cup	red onion, minced
		¼ cup	green onion, minced
1 lb	cooked wild pacific salmon or 4 cans of wild salmon	1 cup	organic oats
		3 tsp	lemon zest
1 tsp	sea salt or to taste	½ tsp	dried chilies
½ tsp	fresh ground pepper	2 tbsp	fresh dill, chopped
2 cups	cooked black rice	2 tbsp	olive oil

Steam yams until soft and then mash until smooth.

In a large bowl, flake the salmon, season with salt and pepper. Add yams, black rice, onions, oats and mix gently with a heavy, wooden spoon. Add lemon zest, chilies and dill. Taste and adjust any seasonings. Wet hands and form into 2 inch burgers.

Heat olive oil over moderately high heat and cook the burgers until dark brown and crispy. Flip and cook the other side, about 3 minutes per side. When cooked place in a preheated 350° oven and bake for 15 minutes.

CHEF'S TIP:

Steaming helps to preserve up to 70% of the vitamins and minerals in vegetables. By submerging them in boiling water, you lose the majority of those vitamins into the water.

Rising Sun Burgers

Serves 4-5

There always seems to be so many ingredients in my burgers. Don't ask me why, they just seem to work out that way. Serve these little gems with shiitake, tahini sauce (pg.117), stir fried baby bok choy and bitter melon. Soak the beans for 4 hours and then cook for about 1 hour until soft.

¾ cup	dried adzuki beans	¼ cup	red onion, chopped
2 tbsp	sesame oil	1½ cups	cooked brown rice
1 cup	dried shiitake mushrooms	1 cup	carrot, grated
2 cups	mushrooms, chopped	½ cup	daikon radish, grated
1½ inch	piece fresh ginger peeled & minced	4 green	onions, chopped
		¼ cup	tamari
2 large	cloves garlic, minced	1 tsp	mirin
½ large	white onion, chopped	½ bunch	coriander, chopped

In a small saucepan, cover the shiitakes with water, bring to a boil and simmer for 15 minutes. Turn off heat. Cover and let sit for another 15 minutes. Remove mushrooms, drain and chop, discarding the stem.

In a large frying pan cook the mushrooms, ginger, garlic and onions in the sesame oil over medium heat until mushrooms are almost dry. Add shiitakes. Let cool 10 minutes. Put mixture in a food processor and pulse until coarsely chopped.

In a large bowl combine the mushroom mixture together with remaining ingredients. Mix thoroughly. Shape into patties and place on a lightly, sesame oiled baking tray and bake in a 350° oven for 30 minutes.

Sweet Susie Burgers

Serves 2

" I created these burgers in honour of my dear friend Susie Dias, Director of East West Yoga in Toronto. She really is one of the sweetest people I have ever met. I had intended on making a mushroom burger and found that I didn't have any mushrooms. So in a pinch or panic, I came up with these. They were a success and the group asked that they be in my book. "

These burgers work well paired with red beet sauce (pg.118) and served with Ontario corn on the cob with orange oregano butter (pg.129) and a big salad. Or you could put them between black olive buckwheat buns and serve with usual burger fixin's. This recipe doubles and triples easily. Use canned beans if you don't have time to cook them.

⅔ cup	golden beets, grated	¼ cup	organic oats
⅔ cup	carrots, grated	2 tbsp	tamari
⅓ cup	zucchini, grated	1 to 2 tsp	dried thyme
¾ cup	short grain brown rice cooked	¼ tsp	tobasco
¾ cup	adzuki beans, cooked & mashed	¼ tsp	liquid smoke
			sea salt & fresh pepper to taste

Preheat oven to 350°. Lightly oil a baking sheet with sunflower oil.

Squeeze out excess liquid from vegetables and in a large bowl mix all ingredients together. Let sit for half an hour to develop flavours. If burgers are too wet, add more rice and a few more oats. Adjust seasonings to taste. Shape into patties.

Bake for 25 minutes, until crispy on the outside.

Puy Lentil Burgers

Makes 12 healthy patties

Puy lentils are lovely, small and black, grown in Le Puy, France. They have a sweet, earthy flavour and are considered by some as the crème de la crème of lentils. One cup of cooked lentils provides 18 grams of protein, plus iron, potassium and fiber.

2½ cups	puy lentils	1½ tbsp	Braggs
2 cups	acorn squash, cubed	1 tbsp	thyme
2 cups	broccoli, chopped	1 tbsp	Italian seasoning
2 cups	cauliflower, chopped	1 tsp	cajun seasoning
¾ large	red onion, chopped	½ tsp	dried chilies
½	vidalia onion, chopped	½ tsp	seasoned salt
½ cup	oats	½ tsp	dulse

Wash lentils in several changes of water, cover with about an inch of water, bring to a boil and simmer until tender, about 25 minutes. You will need roughly 4 cups of cooked lentils. Drain excess water, let cool.

Steam squash, broccoli and cauliflower in a steamer until tender. Set aside. In a frying pan in 2 tbsp sunflower oil, cook onion until tender. Set aside.

Combine all vegetables including onions in a food processor and pulse until well combined. In a large bowl combine lentils, vegetables, Braggs, oats, and all seasonings. I find the best way to mix the ingredients is with your hands. Taste and adjust seasonings. Form into patties and bake on a lightly oiled baking sheet for about 30 minutes in a 350° oven.

Crab & White Fish Cakes

Makes 7 large cakes

" These are fast and yummy fish cakes which go well paired with home-made tartar sauce (pg.161), fresh garden peas and corn on the cob. Helping me to create these delectable cakes was Andy's beautiful daughter, Shu Wei, on one of her delightful visits to Harmony Dawn. Alaskan pollock, white fish such as haddock or cod work well. I use canned crab for convenience but if you can, use fresh cooked crab (about 2 cups). "

1½ cups	cooked, mashed potatoes	½ tsp	ground black pepper
2 cans	crab meat (7 oz size)	Zest	of 1½ large lemons
1 lb	white fish	3 tsp	dijon mustard
¼ cup	green onions, chopped	½ cup	panko bread crumbs
2 tbsp	fresh dill, chopped	1	egg, whisked
1½ tsp	sea salt	2 tbsp	olive oil

In a frying pan, cover the white fish with water, add 3 bay leaves, pinch of salt and a few peppercorns. Bring to a boil and simmer 10 minutes until just done. With a slotted spoon, gently lift fish from pan removing excess water and pat dry.

In a large bowl add all ingredients except bread crumbs and egg, blending gently with a fork until well combined. Taste and adjust seasonings – you may want to add more dill. Form into even patties.

Set up 2 bowls, one with the panko crumbs, the other with the egg. Working with one patty at a time, dip into egg, (dripping off excess) and then into the breadcrumbs. Set aside while you finish all the patties.

Heat oil in a frying pan until hot, add patties and cook over medium heat until nicely brown on both sides. Serve on a platter garnished with lemon wedges, dill and tartar sauce.

Chili with Cashews

Serves 5-6

This is a wonderfully fragrant and slightly sweet chili. It's versatile and can be served during the week or for dinner parties. The cashews and raisins impart a richness to the sauce. Homemade crusty bread or organic rice and garden greens turn this chili into a highly nutritious and colourful feast.

3 tbsp	unsalted butter	1 tsp	ground cumin
1 large	onion, chopped	2 large	cloves garlic, minced
1	green pepper, chopped	1 tsp	dried basil
2 stalks	celery, chopped	1 tsp	dried oregano
2 cups	cooked, red kidney beans	1	bay leaf
2 cups	tomato sauce	½ tsp	fresh ground pepper
2 cups	cooked corn	1 cup	raisins
2 cups	canned, whole tomatoes	1 cup	whole unsalted cashews
2-3 tsp	chili powder	3 drops	hot sauce

Optional Addition: Grated Monterey Jack or Cheddar Cheese

In a large pot, over medium heat, sauté onion, green pepper and celery in butter until crisp tender, roughly 10 minutes.

Add beans, tomato sauce, corn, tomatoes, chili powder, hot sauce, cumin, garlic, basil, oregano, bay leaf and black pepper. Bring to a boil, reduce heat and simmer over low heat for approximately 30 minutes. Stir in the raisins and cashews and continue to simmer until the raisins are plump and the cashews are tender about 20 minutes.

To serve, ladle into bowls and top each serving with grated cheese if desired.

Chickpea Vegetable Curry

Serves 5-7

Serve the curry with lentil dhal (pg.149) and brown rice or simply on its own. Either way this is a very hearty and satisfying dish. Choose any of the cooling raitas (pg.128) which compliment the heat of the curry. Add 1 cup of coconut milk to make a creamy sauce.

4 cups	cooked chickpeas		1 tsp	paprika
3 tbsp	sunflower oil		¼ tsp	cayenne
1½ tsp	cumin seeds		½ tsp	garam masala
1 large	onion, chopped		1–28 oz	can chopped tomatoes
2 tsp	garlic, minced		2 tbsp	tomato paste
1 tbsp	fresh ginger, grated		1 cup	broccoli & cauliflower chopped
1 tsp	turmeric			
2 tsp	ground coriander		1 cup	swiss chard, chopped

Optional: chopped fresh coriander for garnish

Heat oil in large skillet, add cumin seeds and cook until seeds pop and turn brown. Add onions and garlic and cook until soft, add ginger and remaining spices. Cook for about a minute.

Add tomatoes, tomato paste and chickpeas, simmer until the sauce thickens.

Add remaining vegetables and steam until vegetables are tender and bright in colour. Add salt and pepper and a tablespoon of lemon juice. Stir and serve hot.

Andy's Carrot Arame Tofu Stir-fry

Serves 4-6

" This is one of Andy's magnificent specialities. Simple, satisfying and so good for you. Mineral rich arame, antioxidant rich carrots and ginger, healing shiitakes, protein rich tahini and tofu, and cleansing greens. Wow! An everyday dish or equally appealing for a dinner party. Serve over brown rice or your favourite grain. "

2 cups	dried shiitake mushrooms	½ cup	tamari
2 tbsp	sunflower oil	1 cup	dried arame
1 large	onion cut into slivers	1 pkg	regular tofu, crumbled
2 tbsp	fresh ginger, minced	3 cups	swiss chard, chopped
3 cups	carrots, cut into chunks	1 tbsp	toasted sesame seeds
½ tsp	mirin	2 tbsp	green onions, chopped
½ cup	tahini		

Cover shiitakes with 3 cups of water, bring to a boil, turn off and add 1 tbsp of tamari. Cover and let sit for 30 minutes. Remove from pan and slice, discarding hard stem, reserving broth. In another bowl, cover arame with cold water for 5 minutes, drain and set aside.

In a large frying pan over medium high heat, sauté onions and ginger in oil until golden. Add carrots, shiitakes, arame, ¼ cup of shiitake broth and 2 tbsp tamari.

Make a well in the middle of the pan, add tahini, 2 tbsp shiitake broth, 2 tbsp tamari and stir to mix in with rest of pan. Tahini will thicken the sauce and make it creamy. Add tofu and swiss chard, cooking until heated through. Taste, adjust tamari to taste. Sprinkle with sesame seeds and green onions and serve over brown rice.

Steamed Fish with Black Bean Sauce

Serves 4

Whole steamed fish is always on our menu during festive family occasions. Make sure to purchase whole, scaled and cleaned fish from the fishmonger. Serve this dish surrounded with Asian steamed greens and brown rice.

1 whole	firm white fish about 1 to 1½ lbs, haddock, grouper, snapper or cod
1 tsp	sea salt
2 tbsp	salted black beans, washed & drained
1 tbsp	garlic, minced
2 slices	fresh ginger, shredded
2 tsp	organic soy sauce
¼ tsp	dried chilies or chili paste
2 tsp	sunflower oil
2	green onions, cut into 2 inch strips
1 tsp	corn starch
	fresh coriander sprigs for garnish

Make 3 or 4 slashes to each side of the fish. Rub both sides with salt.

Combine salted beans with ginger, garlic, chilies in a bowl and mash to a paste. Add soy sauce and oil, mixing well.

Rub fish with black bean mixture, place green onions on top. Wrap loosely in foil and place on a pan in oven allowing fish to steam. Bake at 425° for about 15 minutes, depending on thickness of fish, until tender. Lift fish out of foil and place on a platter, reserving juice.

Mix cornstarch with 2 tsp of water and combine with fish juices until thickened. Pour over fish and garnish with coriander.

Kung Po Shrimp

Serves 4

Kung Po is a spicy sauce from northern China. Substitute tofu if you prefer for a vegetarian dish. Serve with stir fried green pepper, eggplant and onions topped with toasted chopped peanuts and a side of basmati rice.

1 lb	medium shrimp, peeled & deveined	⅓ cup	dry sherry or rice wine
¼ cup	cornstarch mixed with ⅓ cup water	2 tbsp	hoisin sauce
		2 tbsp	soy sauce
½ cup	peanut oil	1 tsp	brown sugar
2	green onions, chopped	1 tsp	dried chilies
1 tbsp	ginger, minced	½ cup	toasted peanuts, chopped
2 tsp	garlic, minced		dried chili pods for garnish
	sea salt & fresh pepper		

Dip shrimp in the cornstarch mixture and drain off excess. In a wok heat oil until smoking, add shrimp and fry for about 3 minutes until golden brown. Remove using slotted spoon and drain on paper towels.

Leave 2 tbsp of oil in wok and over medium high heat add green onions, ginger and garlic and stir-fry for about 1 minute. Stir in sherry, hoisin, soy sauce, brown sugar, dried chilies and salt and pepper. Bring to a boil, add shrimp back to wok and heat until thickened.

Serve garnished with toasted peanuts, dried chili pods, and green onions.

Jamaican Jerk Spiced Tofu

Serves 8

Jerk spices are traditionally used on chicken but they work really well to bring flavour to tofu. It can be made mild to scorching hot depending on your level of tolerance, so taste along the way. Serve with rosemary roasted potatoes (pg.92) and a green salad with peach vinaigrette (pg.97).

3 pkgs	extra firm tofu	½ tsp	each, cinnamon and
3 large	cloves garlic, minced		ground nutmeg
3	green onions cut into chunks	¼ cup	fresh orange juice or
1	scotch bonnet pepper		half an orange
1½ tbsp	fresh ginger, chopped	3 tbsp	white vinegar
1 tbsp	maple syrup	1 tbsp	Braggs
1 tsp	each, sea salt, black pepper,	1 tbsp	fresh lime juice
	ground allspice, dried thyme	2 tbsp	sunflower oil

Remove excess liquid from the tofu by placing tofu on a plate lined with a towel and put another plate on top with a can weighing down the plate. Let juices drain out for about 30 minutes.

Using gloves, remove seeds from the scotch bonnet pepper. Be careful, this is where the heat is. Lightly coat a large baking sheet with sunflower oil. Cut tofu into ½ inch steaks and place on sheet.

In a food processor blend garlic, green onions, scotch bonnet, ginger, maple syrup, and all spices to form a thick paste.

Add remaining ingredients and blend thoroughly. Spoon over tofu to cover and marinate for 4 hours. Bake tofu at 350° for 25 minutes and then broil tofu for 5 minutes. Serve garnished with lime wedges and summer flowers.

Grilled Tofu Steaks with Charmoula Sauce

Serves 6

Charmoula is a Moroccan sauce which is basically fresh herbs and spices ground to a paste. It is perfect with tofu but works equally well with white fish. Serve with roasted potatoes or basmati rice, salad and grilled vegetables. You can roast in the oven or on the barbeque in a foil lined pan.

2 pkgs	extra firm tofu	½ cup	fresh coriander, packed
3	cloves garlic, minced	½ cup	Italian parsley, packed
1 tbsp	paprika, preferably sweet	2 tbsp	lemon juice
1 tsp	cumin seeds, toasted	⅓ cup	olive oil
¼ tsp	cayenne pepper		sea salt & fresh ground pepper

Remove excess water from tofu and cut into ½ inch thick steaks (pg.174).

Blend all ingredients, except tofu, in food processor until smooth and well combined.

Preheat oven to 450° and using a lightly oiled pan, lay the tofu steaks side by side and pour sauce over top. Roast for 25 minutes.

CHEF'S TIP:

Charmoula sauce works great as a base mixed with mayo or nayo and spread on baguettes with grilled vegetables for a hearty, healthy sandwich.

Baked Tofu in Peanut Shiitake Sauce

Makes a 9 x 13 inch pan

A chunky peanut sauce infused with ginger, garlic and shiitake mushrooms and baked with tofu. Yum! Serve with the curry sauce poured over it for a lovely Thai dish. Add basmati or black rice and Asian greens for a feast. Substitute green curry paste in the sauce if you prefer.

2 pkgs	extra firm tofu	1 small	hot pepper, minced
3 cups	dried shiitake mushrooms	½ cup	Braggs or tamari
1¼ cups	organic peanut butter, chunky	¼ cup	sunflower oil
		1 tsp	dried chilies
3 tbsp	ginger, minced	½ tsp	sea salt
3 large	garlic cloves, minced	¾ cup	shiitake water

In a large pot, cover shiitakes with water, bring to a boil and simmer for 15 minutes. Turn off heat, cover and let sit for 15 minutes. Let cool and remove mushrooms, chop, discarding stems.

In a food processor blend all ingredients except shiitakes and shiitake water, until well combined. Add shiitakes and pulse until minced, add shiitake water and pulse again.

Cut tofu into ½ inch cubes. Preheat oven to 350°. Lightly oil the pan and place the tofu covered with the sauce. Bake for about 30 minutes until tofu is cooked through.

Coconut Curry Sauce

1 can	unsweetened coconut milk	1 tsp	fish sauce
2 tsp	red or green curry paste	3	kaffir lime leaves
2 tbsp	vegetable stock	1 tsp	brown sugar

In a saucepan combine all ingredients over moderately low heat and simmer for 45 minutes until thickened. Do not allow to boil. For additional heat with red curry paste add 1 tsp of chili paste.

Moroccan Chickpea and Vegetable Tagine

Serves 6-8

A tagine is a type of earthen cooking pot used in northern Africa. They slow cook the stew producing a lovely flavour. I however, don't have one yet so I use a large stock pot. It is still really tasty and flavourful especially if made the day before. Serve over brown rice, millet or your favourite grain.

¼ cup	olive oil	1 cup	cilantro, chopped
3	carrots, thickly sliced	1 cup	Italian parsley, chopped
2	potatoes, thickly sliced	1 cup	dried apricots, chopped
3 large	garlic cloves, chopped	1 cup	Thompson raisins
1	red onion, sliced	2 tbsp	tomato paste
1	white onion, sliced	2–28 oz	cans diced tomatoes
2 small	zucchinis, cut into chunks	4 cups	cooked chickpeas
2 cups	green beans	1 cup	almond slivers, toasted

Optional: 1 cup chopped black olives or 1 cup black mission figs

Spices

2 tsp	turmeric	2 tsp	ground cinnamon
3 tsp	cumin seeds, toasted	1 tbsp	dried chilies
3 tsp	coriander seeds, toasted		sea salt and pepper

Grind toasted spices. In a large pot over medium high heat cook onions until softened, about 8 minutes, add spices and cook another 2 minutes.

Turn heat to medium low and add carrots, potatoes, green beans, tomatoes and paste. Let cook one hour or until vegetables are tender, then add zucchini, chickpeas, apricots and raisins and simmer another 30 minutes. At this point you can turn the heat off and let sit several hours or overnight to blend flavours.

Prior to serving, add cilantro, parsley and toasted almond slivers.

Shrimp & Scallops in Spicy Cashew Sauce

Serves 8

" This dish is perfect for festive occasions. In fact, once, due to lack of space in the fridge from holiday festivities, I had put the glass covered dish on a chair in our office, along with other goodies. Much to our shock, when we went to retrieve the dish, our beloved dog, Bearsie, had managed to pull the dish off the chair without spilling it, removed the lid and was having a feast for one, and loving every spicy morsel. It's funny now, but then... "

This dish always gets rave reviews and requests for the recipe. It is a rich dish loaded with spices and packed full of flavour. Serve over organic brown basmati rice and simple steamed Asian greens.

¼ cup	toasted sesame oil	1 tsp	mirin
25 large	shrimp shelled & deveined	½ cup	dry white wine
1 lb	sea scallops	¼ cup	rice vinegar
2 tbsp	fresh ginger, chopped	3 tbsp	tamari
1½ tbsp	garlic, minced	1 tbsp	coriander, chopped
1½ tbsp	shallots, minced	3 tbsp	lemon juice
1 tbsp	dried chilies	1 cup	unsalted cashews, roasted
1 cup	each, orange, yellow & green pepper, chopped	½ cup	unsalted butter
1	jalapeno, minced	½ cup	green onions, chopped

In a wok or a large skillet, heat the oil over medium heat until hot but not smoking. Add the shrimp and scallops and stir fry for about 3 minutes or until cooked through. Remove with a slotted spoon and set aside. In the remaining oil and juices, stir-fry the ginger, garlic, shallots, chilies, bell peppers and jalapeno for about 2 minutes.

Add the mirin, wine, vinegar, tamari, fresh coriander, lemon juice and any juices that have accumulated from the shrimps. Bring to a boil and simmer the mixture until it has been reduced to half.

Add the cashews and whisk in the butter a little at a time. Return the shrimps and scallops to the skillet and cook them over medium heat for about a minute. Transfer to a serving dish, garnish with green onions and serve with basmati rice on the side.

CHEF'S TIP:

You can omit the butter if you like, however, the addition of butter will produce a richer texture and bring all the flavours in the dish together.

Autumn Root Vegetable Pot Pie

Serves 6-8 or a 9 x 13 inch pan

"This is a savoury pie that is wonderful during the autumn and winter months. Although there are many ingredients and steps, it is well worth the effort, as the root vegetables sweeten the savoury sauce, making it comfort food. Serve with salad greens and hearty, earthen bread. This recipe works equally well with tempeh, which will give a stronger, meatier flavour. Prepare as you would the tofu."

Pie Ingredients

Chilled pastry to cover (pg. 29)		7 cups	assorted vegetables:
1 pkg	firm tofu cut into ½ inch cubes		carrots, squash, rutabaga, parsnips
2 tbsp	Braggs		sweet potato, acorn
3 tbsp	sunflower oil		squash, potatoes
1 cup	chopped onions	1 cup	peas
½ cup	chopped celery	1 cup	corn
1 tsp	sea salt	1 cup	sliced mushrooms

Sauce Ingredients

⅓ cup	all-purpose flour	2 tsp	dried marjoram
¼ cup	Braggs	1 tsp	dried basil
¼ cup	tahini	1 tsp	dried sage
1 tsp	light miso	1 tsp	dried rosemary
½ cup	nutritional yeast	2	bay leaves
5 cups	vegetable stock		sea salt & pepper to taste

Preheat oven to 400°.

In a small bowl combine tofu and Braggs. Lightly oil a baking sheet with sunflower oil and place tofu on sheet. Bake approximately 25 minutes until crispy, turning once. Turn oven down to 350°.

Heat remaining oil in a large stock pot over medium heat. Add onions and cook until tender. Add celery and root vegetables and cook, stirring frequently until al dente (still a bit firm) approximately 20 minutes. You may need to add a tbsp or so of water to prevent sticking. Add peas, corn and mushrooms and turn heat to low. Remove pastry from refrigerator.

In another pot over medium low heat, combine flour, nutritional yeast, Braggs and tahini and blend with a wooden spoon. It will be thick. Add herbs and blend another minute. Add stock and whisk until thickened, making sure there are no lumps.

Add seasoned stock mixture to vegetable pot, combine well and cook over low heat for 10 minutes. Remove from heat and pour into the pan.

Roll out chilled pastry on a lightly floured board and press pastry over pan, reserving any extra pastry for decorations. Cut an X in the centre to allow the steam to release.

Make an egg wash using one whisked egg and one tbsp of water and brush on pastry. Place in the middle of the pre-heated oven and bake until golden brown, approximately 25 minutes. Remove from heat and let sit 5 minutes before cutting.

Creamy Fish & Shellfish Pie

Serves 8

" This is such a wonderful and versatile dish, perfect for holiday occasions or small dinner parties. The puff pastry adds a real flair but this dish can also be served as a stew. The best white fish to use is cod, but halibut works equally as well. "

1	onion, minced	½ tbsp	fresh thyme, minced
1	rib of celery, sliced thin	½ tbsp	fresh basil, minced
½	fennel bulb, sliced into segments	½ cup	heavy cream, plus 2 tbsp
		3 tbsp	cornstarch
2 tsp	garlic, minced	1½ lbs	white fish of choice
2 tbsp	olive oil	¾ lb	sea scallops, halved
½ tsp	fennel seeds	¾ lb	each, shrimp & calamari
1 cup	bottled clam juice	2 tbsp	Italian parsley, minced
2 cups	fire roasted tomatoes		sea salt & fresh pepper
¼ tsp	dried chilies	1 pkg	puff pastry, thawed
¼ lb	mushrooms, sliced		

In a large pot over medium heat, add the olive oil, onion, celery, fennel, mushrooms and garlic, stirring until onion is softened. Add fennel seeds, clam juice, tomatoes, thyme, and basil and simmer for 15 minutes. Peel and devein shrimp and slice white fish into chunks. Wash scallops and calamari.

In a small bowl whisk together the cornstarch and cream making sure there are no lumps. Add the mixture to the pot, whisking for about a minute (it will thicken nicely).

Stir in the seafood, parsley, salt and pepper. Remove from heat and transfer to a baking dish.

On a floured surface roll out the puff pastry and fit over the dish leaving a one inch over hang. Use any extra pastry to decorate the top of the pie. Cut an X in the middle to allow steam to escape.

Brush the pastry with the reserved 2 tbsp of cream and place in the middle of a preheated 425° oven for about 20 minutes, until the crust is puffed and golden.

CHEF'S TIP:

You can substitute ½ tsp dried herbs for the fresh. Try to choose white fish that aren't on the endangered species list; avoid seabass and orange roughy.

7
DESSERTS

The Story of Lucy's Lemon Squares

I wrote this recipe when I was about 7 or 8 years old. During the fun process of writing my book, I was visited at the retreat by my mom and 3 of her friends, Joan, Betty and Marcela. I have known Joan and Betty since childhood as they worked with my mom. Joan's daughter Heather has been a friend now for about 35 years.

I had not seen them in years and over lunch and girl talk, I mentioned I was writing a book. Out of the blue, Joan shared that she had recently found this old recipe, which I had made for her when I was a child. She had kept it all these years in a safe place preserved between plastic. She loved the lemon squares then and I love that she kept it and treasured it as she did. They are still yummy little gems. I have included an easier to read version along with the 1970 original just for fun.

LUCY'S LEMON SQUARES.

i cup flour all purpose. ½ cup butter. ¼ cup powdered sugar. sift flour and sugar into bowl. blend in butter with clean fingertips until well mixed. pat evenly into the bottom of an 8 x 8 inch baking pan. bake for 20. minutes at 350°. meanwhile, beat togeth-

er: ~~XXXX~~   2 eggs
1 cup granulated suger
1/2 teaspoon baking
pouder. 2 1/2 tablespoon
fresh lemon juice.
dash of salt. pour
over baked crust
and return to oven
for 20-25 minutes
at same temperature.
cool on rack. cut squares. sprinkle with
sifted, powdered
suger

Lucy's Lemon Squares ~ 2007

Makes an 8 x 8 inch pan

1 cup	all-purpose flour
½ tsp	baking powder
½ cup	unsalted butter
¼ cup	powdered sugar
2	eggs
1 cup	granulated sugar
2½ tbsp	fresh lemon juice
1 tsp	lemon zest
dash	of sea salt

Sift together flour and baking powder, sugar and salt. Blend in butter until well combined. Pat evenly into the bottom of an 8 x 8 inch pan. Bake for 20 minutes in a 350° oven.

Meanwhile, beat together eggs, sugar, lemon juice and zest. Pour over baked crust and return to oven for 20-25 minutes. Cool on a rack. Sprinkle with sifted powdered sugar and cut into squares.

Apple Pear Crisp with Maple Cream

Serves 8-12 or a 9 x 13 pan

> " I love fruit desserts. The natural sweetness of the fruit comes out in baking so you don't need a lot of extra sweetness. In fact you can omit the maple syrup entirely and simply use butter and cinnamon for the crust. The beauty of fruit crisps is that they are prepared according to what is in season. Yum! "

Serve this crisp on its own, with the maple cream or with organic french vanilla ice cream. Use Ontario pears and apples when in season, which will take this dish into the realm of absolute yumminess!

Crisp Ingredients

6	Royal Gala apples, cored & sliced in ½ inch pieces	2 tsp	grated orange zest
4 to 6	Anjou pears, cored & sliced in ½ inch pieces	¾ cup	cranberry juice
		1 tbsp	cornstarch
1 cup	fresh cranberries	1 tbsp	anise seeds
¼ cup	flour, any type	1 tsp	freshly grated nutmeg

Topping

2 cups	organic oats
½ cup	unsalted butter, melted
½ cup	maple syrup or brown sugar
1 tsp	cinnamon

Preheat oven to 350°. Butter a 9 x 13 baking dish and set aside.

In a large bowl, toss together the apples, pears, cranberries, flour, nutmeg and orange zest.

In a separate bowl, combine the cornstarch, cranberry juice and anise seeds and pour over the fruit mixture. Place in prepared pan.

In a separate bowl combine all topping ingredients and gently cover the top of the fruit mixture. Cover with foil and bake for 30 minutes, remove foil and bake for an additional 25 minutes. Let rest for 5 minutes before serving.

Maple Cream

1 pkg   silken tofu
½ cup   maple syrup or to taste
1 tsp   vanilla extract

Blend all ingredients in blender until completely smooth. Place in the refrigerator until needed, (this will thicken the cream slightly).

Maple Almond Cream

Prepare as above but substitute 1 tsp almond extract for the vanilla.

Summer Peach and Berry Crumble

Serves 6-8 or an 8 x 8 pan

This dessert really captures Ontario's summer bounty and it is so fragrant when baking. Try other fruit and nut combinations, you really can't go wrong. Try to use whole spices and grind as required; they make a world of difference. Serve with maple almond cream (pg. 191).

3 cups	Ontario peaches	1 tsp	cinnamon
2 cups	Ontario wild blueberries	½ tsp	ground nutmeg
1 cup	Ontario strawberries	½ tsp	ground cardamom
1 cup	all-purpose flour	½ tsp	sea salt
1½ cups	organic oats	½ cup	unsalted butter, melted
¾ cup	almond slivers, toasted	1 tsp	vanilla extract
⅓ cup	maple syrup	½ tsp	almond extract

Preheat oven to 350° and butter an 8 x 8 baking dish.

Removing the skins from the peaches is easy. Score an X in the base of the peach with a sharp knife and drop into boiling water for 3 minutes. Remove and drop into ice water. The skins will slip off.

In a large bowl combine the peaches and berries and stir in ¼ cup of flour to coat.

In another bowl combine the oats and all remaining dry ingredients. Mix in the butter, vanilla and almond extract. Combine thoroughly.

Scoop fruit into the buttered dish and cover with the oat mixture. Bake until the fruit is bubbling and the crust is golden brown. Can be served hot or at room temperature.

Decadent Chocolate Brownie Cake

Serves 8-12 or a 9 x 13 pan

" I take the inspiration for this recipe from my dear friend Moira Nordholt, whom I adore. She blessed my kitchen and my guests with her version of this cake and I have since created my own rendition. To my gypsy friend whose popularity among chocolate connoisseur's reigns supreme. I thank you from the bottom of my heart. "

This is a fabulous, dense, chocolate brownie cake. Ice with chocolate icing (pg.199) or maple almond icing (pg.191) and garnish with edible summer flowers. Substitute carob chips for a vegan alternative.

1½ cups	chopped dates	⅓ cup	maple syrup
½ cup	water	1 cup	premium dutch cocoa
14 oz	semi-sweet chocolate, chopped	2 ripe	bananas
		2 pkgs	silken firm tofu

Optional: 1 cup toasted walnut pieces, chopped

In a large skillet, bring water and dates to a boil. Simmer over low heat until the dates have turned to a thick paste. Add the chocolate chips, cocoa and maple syrup and simmer until melted and combined. Remove from heat.

Blend the tofu and bananas in a food processor until smooth and creamy. Add to the pan with the other ingredients.

Pour into a lightly oiled pan and bake at 350° for 35 to 40 minutes or until firm and set and cake pulls away from edge of pan.

Lemon Feather Cake

Makes one 9 inch round cake

" This is a lovely, light cake, perfect after a heavy meal. The addition of the potato flour makes the cake so light and airy. Use lemon curd mixed with whipped cream or silken tofu for the icing. Top the cake with fresh raspberries and edible flowers and serve with raspberry coulis (pg.214). "

Meyer's lemons are a cross between a lemon and a Mandarin orange. They have a really unique flavour. If unavailable, regular lemons will work just fine.

1 cup	unsalted butter	½ cup	potato flour
1¼ cups	organic cane sugar	2 tsp	baking powder
5 large	eggs		pinch of sea salt
grated	zest of 3 Meyer's lemons, reserving juice	2 cups	lemon curd (pg.195)
		1 cup	heavy cream, whipped or
1¼ cup	all-purpose flour	1 pkg	silken tofu, blended

Preheat oven to 350° and butter a 9 inch cake pan.

Using a mixer or KitchenAid, beat the butter and sugar until light and fluffy, about 5 minutes. Beat in eggs one at a time. Add lemon zest, reserving juice.

In a separate bowl, mix together the dry ingredients. Fold into the egg mixture. Spoon into cake pan and bake 45 to 50 minutes until a tester comes out clean. Remove from pan when cake has cooled.

Cut cake in half horizontally. Mix together the lemon curd and whipped cream/ tofu and place in the middle, on the top and around the sides. Garnish with raspberries and pansies.

Fresh Lemon Curd

Makes about 2 cups

Lemon curd is amazing and versatile. It's great to have on hand to use as a topping for scones, muffins or ice cream. Mixed with whipped cream or silken tofu, it becomes a lovely mousse dessert called a lemon fool. Keeps for about 2 weeks refrigerated.

1 cup	organic cane sugar or sucanet
½ cup	unsalted butter
2 tbsp	freshly grated lemon zest
¼ cup	lemon juice
3	eggs, beaten well

Combine all ingredients in a heavy pot. Stir gently over low heat until the mixture coats the back of a spoon, about 7 minutes. Do not let boil as it will curdle.

Remove from heat, cool and refrigerate until needed.

Key Lime "Cheesecake"

Makes one 10 inch round cake

" This dessert is inspired by, and dedicated to, my very dear friend and designer of my cookbook, Sharon Buchanan. A passionate and talented teacher of the arts, she came out to help me one weekend and much to our surprise, we found key limes locally. Our eyes locked. "Wow! Key limes, yum!" The rest was a mutual taste test with hers being the seal of approval. "

Key limes are lovely small limes that are packed full of sun loving flavour. You can find them in specialty markets.

Base

3 cups	graham crackers
½ cup	melted butter
2 tsp	pure vanilla extract

Filling

2 pkgs	silken firm tofu
1¼ cups	organic raw cane sugar
3 tbsp	key lime zest
Juice	6 key limes

For the Base

Combine all ingredients in a bowl and press into the base and sides of a buttered 10 inch spring form pan. Bake in a preheated 375° oven for 15 minutes, until golden brown. Remove and let cool.

For the Filling

In a food processor, blend the tofu until smooth and creamy. Add the sugar and blend three minutes, until sugar is dissolved. Add zest and juice, continue blending until well combined. Taste. Add more lime zest until desired level of tartness is reached.

Pour filling into base and bake in a preheated 375° oven for about 50 minutes until solid. Remove from oven and let cool completely.

To serve, garnish with key limes slices and edible pansies.

Chocolate Earth Cake

Makes 2 round eight inch cakes

" This is one of the most popular desserts at Harmony Dawn. It actually feels good when you eat it—not too sweet, dense and bursting with the essence of chocolate, bananas and dates. It's great for birthdays, with chocolate icing or tuck home-made raspberry preserves between the layers. A discovery made by lovely Jen and Cara at one of my cooking workshops. "

This recipe works beautifully with spelt flour or whole wheat. For a change try carob powder and carob chips. The texture will change slightly but it will still be yummy.

1 cup	organic applesauce		1½ cups	dutch process cocoa
2	ripe bananas, mashed		1½ cups	all-purpose flour
½ cup	water		2 tsp	baking powder
1½ cups	dates, chopped		1 tsp	baking soda
2 tsp	ground flax seed		½ tsp	sea salt
½ cup	maple syrup		1½ tsp	cinnamon (optional)
1 cup	chocolate chips			

Butter and dust the pans with cocoa, set aside. Preheat oven to 350°.

Mix the applesauce and bananas together. In a separate bowl sift dry ingredients together.

In a large skillet, combine water with ground flax and dates, stirring over medium low heat until dates turn creamy. Add maple syrup and chocolate chips and stir until melted. Add apples and banana mixture and stir until well combined.

Add dry ingredients to wet and stir until just combined.

Pour into prepared pans and bake for about 40 minutes until the sides pull away from the pan and a toothpick comes out fairly clean. This is a dense cake, earthy and substantial.

Let cool, remove from pans and ice with chocolate tofu icing or leave plain and serve with fruit.

Chocolate "Icing"

1 pkg	silken tofu
1 cup	chocolate chips, melted
1 tsp	vanilla extract

Blend together until smooth. Taste and add a tbsp of maple syrup if you prefer it sweeter. Put into refrigerator until set (about 1 hour) and then ice the cake.

Caramelized Lemon Tart

Serves 12

" This tart is an all time favourite. It is so light and tart that you only need a sliver to satisfy. I have served it on its own or with a teaspoon of raspberry coulis (pg.214) for an elegant finish to a meal. The pastry is made with vanilla and lemon, which adds a subtle sweetness to the flavour. "

Pastry

2 cups	white pastry flour
2 tsp	organic sugar
½ tsp	sea salt
½ tsp	fresh lemon zest
1 cup	chilled, unsalted butter, cut into bits
1 tsp	vanilla

Custard Filling

6 large	eggs
1 cup	plus 2 tbsp, organic sugar
6 tbsp	unsalted butter
⅓ cup	heavy cream
¾ cup	lemon juice
1 tsp	fresh lemon zest
⅓ cup	brown sugar

To Make Pastry Shell

Using a food processor, combine all ingredients. Pulse until it resembles coarse meal. Add the vanilla and 2 tsp of ice water, (1 tsp at a time), until the dough holds together to form a ball. Dust lightly with flour and chill, wrapped in waxed paper for one hour.

Roll the dough on a floured surface into an ⅛ inch round and fit into a 10 inch tart pan. Prick the bottom of the shell with a fork and chill for 30 minutes.

Preheat oven to 325°. Line the shell with waxed paper and fill with rice or beans. Bake in the lower third of the oven for 15 minutes, or until lightly golden. Remove the rice and paper carefully and bake for 10 more minutes, until golden. Let cool slightly.

To Make Filling

In a saucepan over medium heat, whisk eggs and sugar until blended thoroughly. Whisk in butter, cream, lemon juice and zest and whisk for 10 minutes until thickened. Do not allow to boil. The mixture should be able to coat the back of a spoon.

Pour the filling into the tart shell and bake in 325° oven for 15 to 25 minutes until set and the crust is lightly golden. Remove from oven. You can caramelize the tart now or wait until you are ready to serve.

Turn oven to broil, sprinkle the tart with brown sugar and broil until caramelized, about 4 minutes. Be careful not to burn the crust, (it happens very easily). Let the tart cool and then remove from pan. Decorate with raspberries and calendula flower petals and serve.

Mango Lime Brûlée Tart

Serves 10

This dessert is very easy to make. It is light with a Caribbean flare. It's best served the day it is made. Use mangoes that are ripe but not overly juicy.

Base

1½ cups	organic oats
½ cup	spelt flour
¼ cup	melted, unsalted butter
¼ cup	maple syrup
	pinch of sea salt

Filling

2 large	mangoes, ripe but firm to the touch
1 pkg	silken tofu
1 cup	organic sugar
1 to 2	limes, zested

Lightly butter a 9 inch spring form pan. Set aside. Preheat oven to 325°

In a food processor or blender, blend oats until fine. In a medium bowl, combine well, the oats, flour, salt, butter and maple syrup. Press into pan and bake for 10 minutes until set. Remove and prepare filling.

Skin mangoes, remove fruit and purée in a food processer with tofu, sugar and limes until smooth, with no lumps. Taste, adjusting sweetness if necessary.

Pour into pan and bake approximately 40 minutes until set. Allow cake to cool completely, unrefrigerated. If refrigerated the tart will sweat and become too moist.

Sprinkle with brown sugar and broil until caramelized. Decorate and serve with fruit granita (pg.212), fruit coulis (pg.214) or vanilla ice cream.

Date Energy Nuggets

Makes about 40 confections

"The inspiration for these little gems came from my friend, Susie, who mentioned to me that she once ate a cocoa-date delicacy while on a meditation retreat. Hmmm, I thought, sounds yummy. This is my version and much to my delight, my father Derek, a chef in his own right who loves taste tests and giggling, helped me create this recipe."

These are an energy boosting little nugget. Coconut, raisins, almond butter and tahini are protein packed for that afternoon slump. Omit the chocolate and substitute chopped toasted almonds for a change.

1 cup	minced, pitted dates	¼ cup	almond butter
2 cups	organic brown rice crispies	¼ cup	tahini
2 cups	unsweetened macaroon coconut plus ½ a cup	1 tsp	pure vanilla extract
		1 tsp	rice syrup
¾ cup	Thompson raisins	¼ cup	chocolate chips

In a large bowl gently combine dates, rice crispies, coconut and raisins, being careful not to crush the rice crispies.

In a saucepan over medium low heat, combine remaining ingredients until smooth and creamy and chocolate is melted. Add to the dry ingredients. I have found that using my hands works better than a spoon.

In a small saucepan, toast remaining ½ cup of coconut. Roll into 1 inch balls and then roll in the toasted coconut. Refrigerate for one hour until set.

Spice Cookies

Makes 2 to 3 dozen

These cookies have a lovely, soft texture that is almost cake like, with a spicy molasses taste. They are hearty, yet satisfying and simple, with minimal sweetness.

2 cups	whole wheat flour plus 2 tbsp	2 tbsp	honey
¼ tsp	ground ginger	¼ cup	sunflower oil
¼ tsp	nutmeg	½ cup	molasses
¼ tsp	cinnamon	½ tsp	baking soda
¼ tsp	allspice	½ cup	tart applesauce
½ tsp	sea salt	¼ cup	packed brown sugar

In a large bowl combine the flour, spices, sea salt and brown sugar. In a separate bowl combine the honey, oil, and molasses. Stir into the flour mixture. In a small bowl combine baking soda and applesauce, (it will start foaming). Add to flour mixture and blend well.

The batter will be firm not wet. Drop dough onto a parchment lined sheet and bake in a 350° oven for about 15 minutes, until the tops are firm to touch. They will have a cake like texture. Remove from pan and cool on a rack.

Honey Oatmeal Cookies

Makes about 3 dozen

"These are probably my all time favourite cookies. They have crunch on the outside, are soft on the inside and are packed with flavour and vitamins. Yet above all, they give you that "sweetie treatie" fix, as my nutritionist friend, Jane Sloan, affectionately says. They are versatile and forgiving. Throw in chocolate chips or carob, change the seeds to almonds; just play, that's what cookies are for..."

½ cup	butter		1 cup	all-purpose flour
½ cup	sunflower oil		¾ tsp	sea salt
½ cup	honey		¾ tsp	baking powder
2 tsp	vanilla extract		½ tsp	cinnamon
½ cup	raisins, chopped		½ tsp	freshly ground nutmeg
½ cup	sunflower seeds, chopped		⅛ tsp	ground cloves
1 cup	whole wheat flour		1 cup	regular oats

Using a hand blender or KitchenAid, cream together the butter, oil and honey. Add vanilla, raisins, sunflower seeds and stir with a wooden spoon. In a separate bowl combine all the dry ingredients. Add to the wet ingredients and blend well. Drop by teaspoonfuls onto a parchment lined sheet.

Bake in a 350° oven for approximately 10 to 12 minutes, turning the pans halfway through baking. Cookies should be golden on the bottom but not brown.

Chocolate Walnut Harmony Cookies

Makes about 30 cookies

Chocolate and walnuts go hand in hand in a cookie. These are a richer cookie than the others in my book but they sure are good. Add apricots or figs for a different taste sensation. I have made these with spelt flour which gives a nice, light texture to the cookie.

¾ cup	unsalted butter at room temperature
¾ cup	brown sugar, sucanet or organic cane sugar
2	eggs at room temperature
1 tsp	vanilla
1 cup	spelt flour
1 tsp	baking powder
½ tsp	sea salt
1 cup	chocolate chips
1 cup	roasted walnuts, chopped

Optional: ½ cup Kalamata figs or dried apricots, chopped

In a food processor, blend the butter and sweetener together until smooth. Add the eggs one at a time, blending until creamy. Add the vanilla.

In a separate bowl, sift flour, baking powder and salt, mixing thoroughly. Add the chocolate, walnuts and optional figs/apricots and mix until combined.

Drop by spoonfuls onto a parchment lined baking sheet leaving 1 inch between cookies. Bake in a 400° oven for 10 minutes, turning the pans midway through baking. Cookies should be golden and soft. They will harden when they are exposed to the air.

Ginger Oat Cookies

Makes 3 dozen cookies

"I love ginger in just about anything; tea, cookies, cakes, curry, the list is endless. These cookies are hearty due to the addition of the oats. Experiment and add more ginger if you like, omit the chocolate, omit molasses and use all honey if you prefer. Feel free. It's just a cookie!"

½ cup	unsalted butter	2 tsp	baking powder
¼ cup	sunflower oil	1½ tsp	sea salt
½ cup	honey	1 tsp	cinnamon
1	egg	1 tsp	ground ginger
¼ cup	molasses	1 tbsp	fresh ginger, minced
2 cups	rolled oats	¼ tsp	ground cloves
1½ cups	whole wheat flour	¾ cup	chocolate chips

Cream together butter, oil and honey, using a food processor or blender. Beat in egg and molasses. In a separate bowl, sift together all dry ingredients, except the oats and fresh ginger. Stir into the butter mixture.

Add oats, ginger and chocolate chips if using. Mix until combined and drop by spoonfuls onto a parchment lined pan leaving at least 2 inches between cookies.

Bake in a preheated 350° oven for about 8 to 10 minutes, until just golden brown.

Macaroons

Makes about 2 dozen

Macaroons are always a favourite; light and crunchy. These contain brown rice crispies that I love to use any chance I get.

3 oz	semi-sweet chocolate
2	egg whites, with a pinch of sea salt
¾ cup	raw organic cane sugar
1 tsp	vanilla extract
1 tsp	coconut extract
1½ cups	unsweetened macaroon coconut
1½ cups	brown rice crispies
½ tsp	cinnamon

Preheat oven to 350°. Line a baking sheet with parchment paper.

Melt chocolate over medium low heat and set aside to cool.

Using a blender, KitchenAid or food processor, whip egg whites and salt until soft peaks form. Gradually add sugar and beat until glossy and sugar is completely dissolved.

In another bowl combine chocolate, vanilla, cinnamon, coconut and rice crispies. Fold in egg whites until evenly coloured.

Drop by spoonfuls onto sheets. Bake until they are firm and dry on the surface, about 15 to 20 minutes.

Nutty Rice Crispie Squares

Makes an 8 x 8 inch pan

" These are not your usual rice crispie squares. Marshmallows, which are an edible oil product, have been replaced with protein packed tahini and barley malt syrup. I have converted the most ardent of so called "traditional" rice crispie fans over to my side of the fence. This recipe is flexible and forgiving. You can add chopped, toasted pumpkin seeds, omit the chocolate chips or add your favourite nut. "

Barley malt syrup is a natural sweetener made from organic sprouted barley. It isn't overly sweet. Substitute brown rice syrup if unavailable.

¼ cup	tahini
¼ cup	barley malt syrup
½ cup	almond butter or peanut butter
1 tsp	almond extract
2 cups	organic brown rice crispies
⅓ cup	carob or chocolate chips
⅓ cup	sliced toasted almonds
⅓ cup	chopped toasted pecans
⅓ cup	toasted, unsweetened coconut

Butter an 8 x 8 inch dish.

In a sturdy, large pot over medium heat, combine tahini, barley malt, almond butter, and almond extract until warm and blended.

Gently mix in remaining ingredients. Place in dish and chill until 1 hour before serving or until set. Cut into squares.

Harmony Dawn Two Bite Brownies

Makes 24

" These are a favourite at Harmony Dawn. They are great for people with allergies as they are gluten and dairy free (if you use carob chips). It's amazing how much satisfying flavour gets packed into two bites. You will never buy retail "two bites" again as they pale in comparison. You will need mini muffin tins for these. "

Potato flour is very light and adds vitamin C, thiamin, iron and potassium. Add chocolate tofu icing (pg.199) if you desire, but it's not necessary.

1	ripe banana
1 cup	unsweetened organic applesauce
1 cup	sucanet or organic cane sugar
¼ tsp	sea salt
¾ cup	dutch processed cocoa powder, sifted
½ cup	each, brown rice flour and potato flour
1½ cups	semi-sweet chocolate or carob chips, melted

Preheat oven to 350° and lightly butter 24 mini muffin tins.

In a large mixing bowl, mash banana with a fork. Mix in applesauce and sucanet until well combined. Add melted chocolate and mix together.

In another bowl combine salt, cocoa powder and flours. Add to the chocolate mixture and stir until just combined. Due to the starchiness of the potato flour, the mixture can harden fast so you will need to work quickly. Scoop into the muffin cups and press down with a fork.

Bake for 20 to 25 minutes until tops are firm but slightly tender. Let cool 5 minutes and remove to cooling rack. The brownies will continue to firm as they sit.

Fruit Salad with Coconut Chocolate Sauce

Serves 2-4

This is such an easy desert to prepare and one that can be made quickly on a week night or for a formal occasion. Layer the fruit in martini glasses with homemade french vanilla ice cream and top with chocolate swirls.

2	bananas, diced
2 cups	fresh Ontario berries (strawberries, blueberries, raspberries or a combination of all three)
½ cup	unsweetened coconut milk
½ cup	semi-sweet chocolate, grated
½ tsp	pure vanilla extract
¼ tsp	pure coconut extract
1 tbsp	maple syrup
¼ cup	unsweetened coconut, toasted

Optional: french vanilla ice cream or mango sorbet

In a small saucepan, heat the coconut milk until just boiling. Whisk in the chocolate, vanilla and maple syrup and simmer until slightly thickened. Remove from heat.

Using martini glasses, start layering the fruit and sauce. Bananas, berries, sauce – bananas, berries, sauce. If using ice cream or sorbet, add into mixture. Top with the toasted coconut, chocolate swirls and an edible flower.

Granita

Makes a 9 x 13 inch pan

"Granita means (pure heavenly) fruit ice. They are light and airy, with flavours ranging from subtle to very bold. Use them as a dessert or between courses to cleanse the palate. They are an inexpensive and refreshing way to use summer's magnificent bounty. The basic technique is the same for all recipes."

Prepare the fruit mixture, pour into a 9 x 13 glass pan. Place in the freezer and scrape with a fork every hour until icy (roughly 4 hours). Simple! If you leave it too long, simply remove from freezer and whirl in the food processor prior to serving.

Tarragon White Wine

3 cups	water
1 cup	fruity white wine
½ cup	organic cane sugar
Juice	of ½ lemon
1 cup	fresh tarragon leaves

Place all ingredients in a saucepan and bring to a boil. Reduce heat and steep over a low simmer for approximately 20 minutes. Strain and let come to room temperature. Place in pan and freeze.

Basil Orange

As above, omitting white wine and tarragon leaves. Add 1 teaspoon of grated orange rind, ½ cup fresh orange juice and 1 cup of basil leaves

Proceed as above.

Mango Lime

2 large   mangoes
juice   of one lime
½ tsp   lime zest

Peel and remove fruit from mangoes. Place fruit, lime juice and zest in food processor or blender and purée until smooth. Place in the pan and follow basic steps until set. Depending on the size of the mangoes, you may need a smaller sized pan.

Espresso Maple

3 cups   strong black coffee, or espresso
1 tsp   vanilla extract
3 tbsp   maple syrup or to taste

Combine all ingredients together. Place in pan and follow basic steps.

Cantelope Banana

½ small   cantelope, about 3 cups
2 small   ripe bananas
½ tsp   lime zest

Purée all ingredients together. Place in pan and follow basic steps.

Berry Fruit Coulis

"I use fruit coulis' when I want to add an intense burst of flavour and vibrant contrast to a dessert. I never sweeten them. They are simply pure condensed fruit heaven. You need only a mere teaspoon per serving. I put the coulis in a small squirt bottle so I can create designs on the plate and use every last drop."

Raspberry Coulis

1 pint of raspberries puréed in the food processor or blender. Push the blended fruit through a sieve lined with cheesecloth to remove the seeds. From one pint you will be left with about ⅓ of a cup of coulis.

Strawberry Coulis

As above using about 1½ cups of strawberries.

Blueberry Coulis

Blueberries are the least labour intensive of the berries. Using 1 cup of wild Ontario blueberries, purée until smooth and add ½ tsp lemon zest. If too thick add a smidge of water to desired consistency.

Mango Lime Coulis

2 ripe mangoes, peeled and fruit puréed in a food processor. Add juice of ½ lime and ½ tsp of lime zest.

Flavoured Lemonades

Lemonade is the quintessential summer beverage. When flavoured with a seasonal berry, it just takes it over the top. During BBQ season in Ontario and the summer heat in full swing, any taste combination goes. Try whatever appeals to you in the heat of the moment. They could not be simpler. If you feel the mixtures could be sweeter for your taste then add a touch of honey or maple syrup.

Strawberry Lemonade

1 can of concentrated Lemonade

Use good quality, low sugar varieties, organic if possible and mix according to package directions. Add 2 cups of fresh puréed Ontario strawberries. Combine well. Garnish with lime slices and fresh strawberry halves.

Raspberry Lemonade

As above, using 1 cup of raspberries instead of the strawberries, except strain the puréed raspberries with a sieve to remove seeds. Garnish with lemon slices.

Watermelon Lemonade

As above using 2 cups of seeded pink watermelon and pink lemonade.

Chocolate Raspberry Truffles

Makes about 20

> I created these for Andy's mom who wasn't allowed to eat anything with refined sugar due to a medical condition and she was craving something sweet. They are different from standard truffles in that they have no cream or chocolate and only a smidge of melted butter. Keep refrigerated until serving as they will soften at room temperature.

½ cup	chopped dates		2 tbsp	melted, unsalted butter
¼ cup	water		½ cup	dutch cocoa, sifted
¼ cup	almond butter		½ tsp	vanilla extract
2 tbsp	rice syrup		1 tbsp	pure raspberry jam
1 tbsp	tahini		1 tbsp	framboise fruit wine (optional)

In a small saucepan, heat dates and water together over medium low heat until dates are smooth and creamy. Add almond butter, rice syrup, tahini and melted butter until combined.

Remove from heat. Add vanilla, cocoa powder, raspberry jam and framboise, combining fully and making sure there are no lumps. Refrigerate at least 4 hours until solid.

Place 2 tbsp of sifted cocoa powder on a plate. Remove pot and begin rolling the truffles in your hands, about 1 tsp per truffle. Make a nice ball, roll in cocoa, place on a plate and refrigerate again until serving.

Crystallized Flowers

Crystallized flowers are great for garnishing pies, cakes and cookies. They are edible and add a professional flare to your desserts, not to mention colour. The process is very easy, but you do need a little patience when dipping so the petals don't break. Flowers will keep 2 days refrigerated in a container.

2 large   egg whites, whipped
½ cup   white fruit sugar

Edible flowers that work well are violas, pansies, johnny-jump-ups, daisies and apple blossoms.

Brush flower head lightly with egg white and then dip into sugar. Shake off excess sugar and place flower on a parchment lined plate. Continue with remaining flowers. Put plate in fridge and allow flowers to crystallize for 2 to 3 hours. Place in a container until ready to use.

Sample Menu Ideas

A question I get asked a lot is, "How do I put together menus?" I think the question is often based on the notion that adopting a vegetarian diet means, "How will I get enough protein and nutrients?" These are valid concerns. However, in most cases, a vegetarian diet includes more than enough protein from beans, tofu or grains, and more fiber than a non-vegetarian diet. I base my menus on colour, feng shui, texture, season and available ingredients.

BREAKFAST & BRUNCH

Maple Pecan Granola with Fresh Fruit & Yoghurt
Crêpes with Asparagus and Brie
Homemade Oatmeal Molasses Bread with Homemade Jams

Oatmeal Porridge with Warm Apples
Banana Pecan Muffins
Scrambled Eggs with Fresh Herbs

LUNCH

Mushroom Gruyère Quesadillas
Arugula Greens with Creamy Tarragon Dressing
Chocolate Walnut Harmony Cookies

Harmony Dawn Brown Rice Sushi
Seaweed Salad
Salad Greens with Tahini Garlic Dressing

Vegetable Extravaganza Wraps
Black Bean and Corn Salad
Harmony Dawn Two Bite Brownies

Sample Menu Ideas

Cashew Chili
Harmony Dawn Cornbread
Salad Greens with Honey Poppyseed Dressing

DINNER
Spring & Summer

Jamaican Jerk Spiced Tofu
Roasted Garlic Herb Potatoes
Organic Greens with Peach Vinaigrette
Homemade Pitas
Caramelized Lemon Tart

Summer Vegetable Tofu Burgers with Beet Sauce
Ontario Corn on the Cob with Oregano Butter
Organic Greens with Toasted Seeds and Roasted Garlic Fig Dressing
Chocolate Earth Cake

Summer Corn Chowder
Mediterranean Chick Pea Salad
Organic Greens with Roasted Shallot dressing
Orange Basil Granita

Autumn & Winter

Red Lentil Dhal with Raita
Chickpea Vegetable Curry
Date Energy Nuggets

Sample Menu Ideas

Baked Tofu in Peanut Shiitake Sauce
Thai Black Rice
Steamed Asian Greens with Black Sesame Seeds
Key Lime "Cheesecake"

Moroccan Chickpea and Vegetable Tagine with Toasted Almond Slivers
Salad Greens with Orange Raspberry Dressing
Funky Flatbread
Chocolate Earth Cake

MACROBIOTIC

Adzuki Bean Stew over Brown Rice
Steamed Broccoli, Cauliflower and Yams with Tahini Dressing
Apple Pear Cranberry Crisp with Maple Cream

Andy's Carrot Arame Tofu Stir-fry over Brown Rice
Steamed Asian Greens with Lemon and Dulse

Miso Soup
Purple Cabbage over Buckwheat Noodles
Nutty Rice Crispie Squares

Suggested Reading & Viewing

BOOKS & NEWSLETTERS

Sugar Blues, William Dufty, Warner Books, 1975

Silent Spring, Rachel Carson, Houghton Mifflin 1962

Beyond Beef: The Rise and Fall of the Cattle Culture, Jeremy Rifkin, Penguin Group, 1992

Fast Food Nation: The Dark Side of the All-American Meal, Eric Schlosser, Houghton Mifflin, 2001

Chew on this: Everything You Don't Want to Know About Fast Food, Eric Schlosser & Charles Wilson, Houghton Mifflin, 2006

The End of Food: How the Food Industry is Destroying Our Food Supply & What We Can Do About It, Thomas F. Pawlick, Greystone Books, 2006

Renewable Energy Handbook: A guide to Rural Energy Independence, Off-grid & Sustainable Living, William H. Kemp, Aztext Press, 2005

The Weather Makers: How We are Changing the Climate & What It Means For Life On Earth, Tim Flannery, Harper Collins, 2005

A Call to Women, The Healthy Breast Program & Workbook, Sat Dharam Kaur, ND, Quarry Press, 2000

Ageless Wisdom Spirituality, Investing in Human Evolution, Andy James, Xlibris, 2003

Suggested Reading & Viewing

The Conscious I: Clarity and Direction Through Meditation, Andy James, Summerville House, 1992

The Essential Tao, Thomas Cleary, Castle Books, 1998

Nutrition Action Healthletter, Centre for Science in the Public Interest, Monthly Newsletter
Email: circ@cspinet.org

MOVIES

Super Size Me, Morgan Spurlock, Samuel Goldwyn Films, 2004

An Inconvenient Truth with Al Gore, Directed by Davis Guggenheim, Paramount Classics, 2006

The Corporation, Mark Achbar, Jennifer Abbott & Joel Bakan, Zeitgeist Films, 2004

Enron: The Smartest Guys in the Room, Alex Gibney, Magnolia Pictures, 2005

Who killed the Electric Car: A Lack of Confidence or Conspiracy, Chris Paine, Sony Pictures 2006

Index of Recipe Titles

Workshops, Books and Info at Harmony Dawn

Harmony Dawn Retreat is located on Rice Lake just 90 minutes northeast of Toronto. This beautiful off-grid retreat is unique in its vision and design. Feng Shui, the ancient Chinese art of placement, has been used to create a noted sense of tranquility and harmonious flow within the retreat building, which is cozily nestled into a hillside and surrounded by meadows and woodland. Solar and wind power as well as other sustainable energy technologies enable it to be independent of outside utilities and away from public roads. The building itself gives guests a rare opportunity to experience first-hand the living conditions of a cleaner, "greener" future.

Harmony Dawn is open year round and facilitates a diverse variety of groups – yoga, meditation, Tai Chi, Qigong, energy work, psychotherapy, drama art and more.

In addition, Nicola Lawrence and Andy James, co-owners of Harmony Dawn, are committed to healthy living and a balanced lifestyle, which is reflected in their own workshops. Their popular cooking workshops teach integrated cooking skills and participants have an opportunity to practice Insight Meditation and Qigong. Group and private workshops are available. Nicola and Andy have been featured in the Toronto Star, Style at Home magazine, Cottage Life magazine, local newspapers and TV. They are sought out for speaking and teaching engagements on meditation, Qigong, spirituality, cooking, breast health and lifestyle.

For more information on upcoming workshops, booking Harmony Dawn for your own retreat or to be put on our mailing list, please contact us through www.harmonydawn.com

To order The Dao of Harmony Dawn Cooking, specialty items such as popular salad dressings, soups, bread, granolas, jams, and seasonal Gift Baskets, contact the author through www.harmonydawn.com